STYLISH INDIAN
IN MINUTES

OVER 140 INNOVATIVE RECIPES

Monisha Bharadwaj has worked as a food consultant in England and India.
Her first book for Kyle Cathie, *The Indian Kitchen*, was short-listed for the
Guild of Food Writers' Book of the Year Award and the André Simon
Award and won the Gastronomische Akademie Deutschlands.

STYLISH INDIAN
IN MINUTES

MONISHA BHARADWAJ

WITH PHOTOGRAPHS BY GUS FILGATE

TED SMART

DEDICATION

This book is especially for my son Arrush who is passionate about food and for my daughter Saayli who finds it impossible to be interested in it at all. I am inspired to innovate by both — either to please one palate or to tempt the other

Design Mark Latter at Vivid Design
Editor Stephanie Horner
Photography by Gus Filgate
Home economy by Annie Nicholls
Printed by Star Standard, Singapore

Monisha Bharadwaj is hereby identified as the author of this work in accordance with Section 77 of the Copyright, Designs and Patents Act 1988.

A Cataloguing in Publication record for this title is available from the British Library.

ISBN 1 85626 486 6

First published in Great Britain in 2002
by Kyle Cathie Limited
122 Arlington Road
London NW1 7HP
general.enquiries@kyle-cathie.com
www.kylecathie.com

This edition produced for
The Book People Ltd
Hall Wood Avenue
Haydock
St Helens WA11 9UL

CONTENTS

INTRODUCTION

I set up my first home in England when I was 22 years old. I had arrived from Bombay and from a household where servants did the shopping, cooking and cleaning. I had never bought or checked groceries and had certainly not cooked on a daily basis. As a graduate of hotel management, my time in my mother's kitchen had been spent whipping up exotic international delicacies such as Poulet Marengo and Tarte Rustique aux Abricots, much to the delight of my family and friends, who would devour my offerings with utmost enthusiasm and relish.

My first few days in England were an eye-opener. There were endless calls to Bombay asking for home recipes and measures. 'Which rice do I use?' or 'Oh no! I can't get fresh coconut here,' and then 'Even if I find one, how do I grate it?'

With time, I have learned that every cook finds a balance of her or his own. As my work and study pressures began to build, I found that I craved home food more and more. I bought several books on Indian cookery but found, to my dismay, that they made Indian food out to be an 'exotic' cuisine that was any good only after hours of soaking, grinding and cooking. I neither had the time nor the inclination to get into these tedious procedures.

My mother had been a busy, successful working woman all her life and I knew that every time she cooked, for parties or festivals, she was able to create miracles in minutes. I began devising my own techniques and tricks. I wanted authentic Indian food, was not willing to compromise on taste or quality, and I wanted it on my table in minutes rather than hours. By this time, I was also entertaining a lot and guess what my friends always asked for? Indian home-cooked food! I soon found that time is inversely proportionate to innovation and I tried out countless recipes using endless variations until I taught myself a style that I was comfortable with.

Needless to say, I'm not the only one who has pared down the fuss and bother of Indian festive cooking. I say 'festive', meaning special or celebratory, whether a meal for two or a gathering of 50, because Indian home cooking has always been relatively straightforward. Today's young home-makers in India are just as keen to find ways to reduce time in the kitchen, using the hours saved to pursue a career, a hobby or to be with the family.

WHAT IS STYLISH INDIAN?

In order to save time and effort, one cannot just put together anything. I strongly believe that a cook must respect authenticity, be committed to nutrition and taste and enjoy presenting food beautifully. Food has to look 'good enough to eat' and must fulfill all nutritive requirements. All too often Indian food outside India has simply meant

a 'curry'. The cuisines of the many states, regional variations, innovations and evolved recipes find no place in the Indian restaurants around the world. In this book, I have put together a collection of recipes that are suited to the modern busy lifestyle and yet are festive and special. All the recipes, some classic, others new, reflect an evolving Indian cuisine that is truer to today's needs.

INGREDIENTS

My experience has taught me to buy the most dewy, the most crisp and most fragrant fruits and vegetables for my kitchen. My meat, poultry, fish and eggs must be the freshest available or I will not buy. I look for prime cuts bursting with goodness. In selecting spices I look for fat, perfumed pods that will create mystery and allure in my cooking. Milk and milk products must be positively straight off the farm. There are a few concessions: I use ready-powdered spices and I am thankful for treasures such as canned beans, tamarind paste and tomato purée.

There is an endless variety of Indian breads, some of which can be bought. These would typically include naans, rotis (also called chapatis), parathas, with or without herbs, and pitta bread. I would say that eat shop-bought breads within two days, but as they freeze well, they can be put into the freezer for about one week.

A word on chillies. I don't often deseed the less hot green chillies as their seeds are not easy to remove. If you don't like your food too hot, just reduce the number of chillies. However, it's slightly different with the red varieties, such as the Kashmiri, which are often in the dish as much to provide colour as heat. If you want to reduce the level of heat without compromising on the colour, I would suggest you do remove their seeds.

A point worth noting is that if you have eaten something containing more chilli than you can bear, reach for your yoghurt-based raita. The capsaicin in chillies is responsible for their heat, which is insoluble in water or beer so neither can help you recover! Yoghurt, on the other hand, neutralizes capsaicin and is most effective at cooling your tongue.

TECHNIQUES

I use my free time to pre-prepare some ingredients to speed up recipes later:

❖ for ginger-garlic paste, I often buy ready pastes and combine them in a ratio of 1:1 so that I just need 1 spoon and 1 bottle. Most Indian recipes call for a bit of both anyway.
❖ roasted cumin powder is a wonderful spice to have in your cupboard as it gives a lift to almost any savoury dish. Simply heat a dry pan and drop in a few tablespoons of cumin seeds. Stir them until they become dark. Grind them to a powder in a coffee grinder or a small blender and store in a dry jar.
❖ many of the recipes involve frying masala pastes and spice powders. Always cook these on a very low heat, or they will burn. A blended spice paste is cooked when the mixture starts to separate from the cooking oil.

My pantry intredients:
❖ cans of beans: red kidney, flageolets, butter beans, chickpeas, cannellini
❖ cans of pineapple
❖ cans of tomatoes – whole peeled plum, chopped, puréed (sold as passata).
❖ cans of evaporated milk, cream, coconut milk, and lentil soup
❖ many kinds of nuts: almonds, pistachios, peanuts, mixed nuts, cashew nuts, pine nuts, almond powder
❖ jars of mint sauce (great stirred into yoghurt as a dip with kebabs, samosas and bhajias) and apple sauce (to go with fritters)
❖ a few kinds of salt – rock, garlic, onion, sea
❖ olive oil infused with garlic or lemon for an instant salad dressing
❖ wholegrain mustard, peanut butter
❖ tamarind paste, dessicated coconut, pickled green peppers
❖ caster sugar, brown cane sugar
❖ spices and mixtures – garam masala, tandoori masala, cardamom pods and cumin seeds (far better to buy the cardamom pods and grind your own powder as and when you need it)
❖ runny honey

EQUIPMENT

You don't need any specialist utensils or cooking pots other than a few different sized, good-quality heavy-based, lidded pans or casseroles. The type that can be used on the hob and then be transferred direct to the oven are most useful, especially as you can begin by frying onions, garlic, spices and pastes in them, then add meat, vegetables, lentils and liquid and bring to the boil — all in one large pot. Indian cooks will have at least one pressure-cooker, which suits this sequence of intense cooking processes perfectly. Many in the West consider the pressure-cooker an old-fashioned device but I find it indispensable, and the dish is cooked in no time at all. If you don't have any all-purpose casseroles or a pressure-cooker, select a large frying pan for the initial frying or browning, then transfer everything to a saucepan or an ovenproof casserole. Do read each recipe carefully, to check the pan you select is large enough to take all the ingredients and the liquid.

In India we use woks (or *kadhai*) in a similar way to the Chinese, for stir-frying and deep-frying. The *kadhai*, made of aluminium, is heavier than a Chinese wok, as it is has to be used over the heat for longer periods without the food burning.

You will need a grinder of some sort. There are powerful electric blenders which can grind dry and wet ingredients to make powders or pastes. For small quantities, a coffee-grinder is a good way to grind spices. Dry-roasted seeds become brittle and can be effectively ground in a mortar in the time-honoured fashion. But an all-purpose food processor, that can grate, chop and knead is increasingly becoming popular in Indian kitchens.

MEASURES

This book is a reflection of my own experience as well as that of many Indians who have now moved towards a way of cooking that is easy and that involves a minimum of fuss. There is no set way of cooking in India, and my methods often don't give an exact cooking time. I would ask that you use your judgement, eyes, and taste frequently. This is, after all, how to cook properly and to gain personal experience and confidence. I hope that this book will inspire my readers to experiment with ingredients and come up with innovative and delicious meals like many modern Indian people do today. The book is for all of us who would like to spend less time in the making of Indian food and more in its enjoyment.

However, do make sure you follow either the metric or the imperial measures I give in each recipe: don't be tempted to mix the two. It is useful to remember that 1 teaspoon = 5g or 5ml and 1 tablespoon = 15g or 15ml.

With the exception of the Indian-style Fried Eggs (page 115) and Fruit Ice Candy Sticks (page 140), all recipes are for four servings.

TRADITIONAL INDIAN COOKING DOES NOT BOAST A GREAT SOUP AND STARTER REPERTOIRE. IN FACT STARTERS ARE OFTEN FOUND AT 'WESTERNIZED' INDIAN RESTAURANTS RATHER THAN IN HOMES, EXCEPT ON SPECIAL OCCASIONS. An Indian meal has all courses served simultaneously, including the sweet. I like to serve soup at dinner parties simply because it is a way of gently enticing the tastebuds and preparing them for the meal to follow.

My chapter on soups and starters has recipes from homes where starters are served or from colder north India, where, as in the West, the climate dictates the necessity of a warming broth. The meat-based cooking of north Indians has delicately flavoured consommés and stocks, served on special occasions, and *shorbas* or cream soups, thickened with flour, smoothed with cream, and eaten with rice. The Raj left a legacy of Anglo-Indian food including Mulligatawny, meaning 'pepper water' (*molaga + tanni*) in Tamil, the language of south India, from where this soup originates. In the south, a spicy *rasam* or thin, highly spiced lentil broth is sometimes served as a soup. In the scorching summer, cool yoghurt-based soups are preferred.

SOUPS
AND
STARTERS

A delicacy from Karnataka on India's west coast, this tangy soup can be served hot or cold. It is sometimes made without the coconut milk for a thinner soup, with a few curry leaves for flavour. It is also eaten mixed with rice. Choose the reddest tomatoes you can find for the best colour.

TOMATOCHE SAAR

spicy tomato soup

Preparation time: 5 minutes

Cooking time: 15 minutes

1 Make a shallow cross on the base of each tomato using a sharp knife. Place them in a pan, along with the chilli, peppercorns, cumin seeds and salt, and just cover with boiling water.

2 When the tomatoes become mushy (this takes about 5 minutes), lift out with a slotted spoon and peel off the skin. Return the flesh to the water. Cool slightly.

3 Whizz the mixture in a liquidizer. Add the coconut milk and adjust seasoning.

4 Heat gently and serve garnished with a sprig of coriander.

300g (10oz) large, fresh
   tomatoes
1 green chilli
6 peppercorns
½ teaspoon cumin seeds

salt to taste
300ml (½ pint) canned
   coconut milk
coriander sprigs
   to garnish

This soup comes from Rajasthan where the intense sun creates multi-coloured mirages. In the dry, tropical heat, this soup is like ambrosia from the heavens. Best served in a flower-filled summer garden to refresh your guests on a hot summer's day!

KHEERE KA THANDA SHORBA

chilled summer cucumber soup

1 Liquidize the cucumber in a blender, then stir in the yoghurt and garlic.

2 Strain through a fine sieve, making sure you squeeze out all the cucumber juice.

3 Whisk in enough water to make up to 600ml (1 pint). Chill. Season with salt and pepper just before serving.

4 Serve garnished with mint and float an ice cube on top.

Preparation time: 15 minutes

1 cucumber, peeled
300g (10oz) natural yoghurt
1 clove of garlic,
   crushed
salt and freshly ground black
   pepper
1 teaspoon fresh mint,
   finely chopped, or
   mint leaves, to garnish

Saffron is considered the spice of the Gods because it is so fragile and pure. Its inclusion in any recipe assures sophistication and celebration. This aromatic and colourful soup adds dash to an Indian meal. It can be made quickly and, as a real treat, garnished with a piece of edible silver foil (varq), available from most Indian grocery shops.

KESARI MURGH KA SHORBA

chicken and saffron soup

1 Heat the oil in a large, heavy-based saucepan and add the cumin seeds.

2 As they darken, add the cubed chicken and peppercorns and stir until the chicken turns opaque.

3 Add the stock and salt and bring to the boil.

4 Reduce heat and simmer until the chicken is cooked.

5 To serve, shred the chicken into the bottom of warmed individual bowls and pour in the soup. Sprinkle a pinch of saffron strands over each one (the soup should turn a delicate orange). Serve hot.

1 teaspoon sunflower oil
½ teaspoon cumin seeds
300g (10oz) cubed, boneless chicken
½ teaspoon crushed peppercorns
750ml (1¼ pints) chicken stock
salt
¼ teaspoon saffron strands

Preparation time: 10 minutes Cooking time: 15 minutes

PANEER BHARE AVOCADO

avocado filled with cottage cheese

Preparation time: 10 minutes

1 Cut to the middle of the avocados from the stalk end, easing around the stone. Twist both halves carefully and lift apart. Remove stone. Brush the surface with lemon juice to prevent discoloration.

2 Fill each avocado half with the pineapple cottage cheese and chill.

3 To serve, sprinkle with rock salt, roasted cumin powder and chilli powder. Place each avocado half on a mixture of red and green salad leaves.

2 large avocado pears

1 teaspoon lemon juice

150g (5oz) cottage cheese with pineapple

rock salt to sprinkle

¼ teaspoon roasted cumin powder

pinch of chilli powder

mixed lettuce leaves, to serve

CHEESE AUR MIRCH KA TOAST

chilli cheese toast

Preparation time: 5 minutes

Cooking time: 5 minutes

1 Lightly mix the cheese and the chilli.

2 Toast the bread and spread with butter. Divide the cheese mixture between the four slices and spread to cover. Season with salt and pepper. Place under a hot grill until the cheese begins to melt and turns golden brown.

3 Cut each slice into four triangles and serve with curly lettuce on the side.

175g (6oz) Cheddar cheese, grated

1 fresh green chilli, finely chopped

4 slices bread

25g (1oz) butter

salt and pepper

lettuce leaves, to garnish

A tangy, crisp starter from the north of India, best eaten with finely sliced onion rings. In Bombay this dish is so popular that it is sold from many street stalls – in the evening it is not uncommon to see people standing around a handcart

FISH AMRITSARI

Punjabi fried fish with lemon

1 Mix the ginger-garlic paste, lemon juice and rock salt and marinate the fish in the mixture.

2 In a separate bowl, combine the gram flour, ajowan, egg and chilli powder with water to make a thick batter.

3 After 20 minutes, lift the fish out of the marinating mixture and coat each fillet with batter.

4 Heat the oil in a large, heavy-based frying pan and fry the fillets until crisp.

5 Serve hot with lemon wedges.

Preparation time: 10 minutes + 20 minutes marinating
Cooking time: 10 minutes

1 teaspoon ginger-garlic paste
1 tablespoon lemon juice
rock salt to taste
4 fillets of fish (cod or
  similar firm white fish)
2 tablespoons gram flour
pinch ajowan (ajwain)
1 egg
½ teaspoon very red mild chilli
  powder
sunflower oil for deep-frying
lemon wedges, to serve

Ratnagiri is not too far from Bombay. It is lush with coconut trees and enjoys a rich seafood cuisine. In India, crabs, caught from the sea as well as from the many rivers, are plentiful and are quite cheap. This recipe combines the key ingredients from the area. I love it for its sheer glamour, and often use ready-dressed crab to save the bother of cleaning fresh ones.

KHEKDA RATNAGIRI

garlic pepper crab

1 Remove all the crabmeat from the shells and pincers, taking care to extract any tiny bits of shell. Mix together the white and the brown meats. Thoroughly rinse the shells and leave to drain.

2 Heat the oil in a saucepan and add the mustard seeds. When they begin to pop, add the onion and stir until translucent.

3 Add the curry leaves and garlic paste. Stir.

4 Add the coconut and crabmeat and stir lightly until heated through. Season to taste.

5 Pile the mixture into the cleaned crab shells, garnish with some chopped coriander if liked and serve warm on a bed of lettuce.

4 freshly cooked crabs, shells reserved
2 tablespoons sunflower oil
¼ teaspoon mustard seeds
1 medium onion, finely chopped
5 curry leaves
½ teaspoon garlic paste
1 tablespoon desiccated coconut
salt and freshly ground black pepper
freshly chopped coriander leaves, lettuce leaves, optional

Preparation time: 10 minutes   Cooking time: 10 minutes

MURGI NA FARCHA
parsi-style fried chicken

1 Mix the tomato purée, garam masala powder, ginger-garlic paste, chilli powder and salt.

2 Place the chicken drumsticks in a saucepan, cover with the tomato-spice mixture and a few tablespoons of water. Cook for about 10 minutes over high heat, then reduce the heat when the mixture begins to boil, turning occasionally, until the chicken is three-quarters done.

3 Cool, then roll each drumstick first in breadcrumbs, then in beaten eggs and deep-fry in hot oil until crisp and golden brown in a deep-sided, heavy-based frying pan or wok. Drain on kitchen paper.

4 Serve hot, with tomato ketchup, if liked.

4 tablespoons tomato purée
½ teaspoon garam masala powder
2 teaspoons ginger-garlic paste
½ teaspoon chilli powder
salt
8 chicken drumsticks, skinned
40g (1¾oz) fresh breadcrumbs
2 eggs, beaten
sunflower oil for deep-frying

Preparation time: 10 minutes   Cooking time: 25 minutes

MANPASAND SEEKH
skewered lamb in spices

1 Combine all the ingredients except the lamb in a large bowl and mix well. Add the lamb, stir to coat, and marinate the mixture overnight.

2 The following day, thread the lamb pieces onto skewers and cook under a hot grill, turning frequently, for 10–15 minutes or until the meat is cooked. Baste occasionally with the marinade.

3 Heat the remaining marinade in a saucepan and serve it as a dipping sauce.

150ml (5fl oz) natural yoghurt
1 small onion, grated
1 teaspoon garam masala powder
1 teaspoon ginger-garlic paste
1 teaspoon chilli powder
salt to taste
300g (10oz) lean lamb steak,
   diced

Preparation time: 15 minutes + overnight marinating   Cooking time: 15 minutes

This simple starter is a glamorous whirl of colour and texture and tastes especially fresh and clean. It is wonderful for lunch and can easily be made well in advance. It is delicious in the summer with some crusty bread, but it also looks delightful in the winter if you can find some really good out-of-season tomatoes. An added bonus is that it is so simple to make!

TAMATER MAHAL

tomato castles

1 Place 8 of the thickest slices of tomato on a serving plate. Top each one with a slice of cheese, then a couple of slices of avocado and red onion, and build up the layers until all the ingredients are used, to make the castle effect.

2 Combine all the ingredients for the dressing and mix well. Drizzle the dressing over the tomato castles, and serve with warm, crusty garlic bread.

Preparation time: 10 minutes

300g (10oz) large, very red beef tomatoes, thickly sliced

150g (5oz) mozzarella cheese or similar, such as mild Cheddar, sliced

1 ripe, firm avocado, medium sliced

1 medium red onion, sliced

FOR THE DRESSING

2 tablespoons sunflower oil

2 tablespoons lemon juice

½ teaspoon honey

¼ teaspoon coarsely ground black pepper

¼ teaspoon dry ginger powder

salt to taste

1 teaspoon finely chopped coriander leaves

PALAK ALOO BHAJIA

spinach and potato fritters

1 Combine all the ingredients except the oil in a bowl and add enough water to make a thick batter.

2 Heat the oil in a large, heavy-based frying pan and drop in a tablespoonful of mixture. Cook, turning, until lightly browned on both sides. Drain on kitchen paper and keep warm while you make the rest.

3 Continue to fry the fritters in batches until the batter is used up, and serve hot.

Preparation time: 10 minutes

225g (8oz) fresh spinach leaves, chopped
150g (5oz) grated potato
½ teaspoon ground nutmeg
75g (3oz) gram flour
salt and pepper to taste
sunflower oil for deep-frying

METHI MUTHIYAS

baked fenugreek crispies

1 Combine all the ingredients in a mixing bowl and knead into a soft dough, using a little water.

2 Divide the dough into 8 equal portions, mould into longish, barrel shapes on your palm.

3 Place on a greased baking tray and bake in a preheated oven (200°C/400°F/gas 6) for about 8 minutes, or until crisp and golden in colour.

4 Serve hot with a wedge of lemon.

Preparation time: 10 minutes   Cooking time: 8 minutes

1 tablespoon dried fenugreek leaves
5 tablespoons wholewheat flour
5 tablespoons gram flour
¼ teaspoon ginger paste
¼ teaspoon garam masala
1 teaspoon sugar
1 tablespoon sunflower oil
salt
lemon wedges, to serve

Mushrooms are a recent addition to the Indian vegetable market. Now they are so popular that vast farms have developed for their cultivation. Indian recipes usually call for button or white mushrooms. This one is an easily put together dish for unexpected visitors. Its simplicity and spicy flavour make it a favourite cocktail snack or starter.

MASALA MUSHROOMS

mushrooms with chilli and garlic

1 Combine the chilli powder, garlic paste, cumin powder, oil and salt in a bowl. Add in the mushrooms and lightly stir until well coated.

2 Spread the mushrooms on a heatproof tray and grill under medium heat for a few minutes until they soften and turn slightly dark. Serve hot with wedges of lemon.

Preparation time: 10 minutes

¼ teaspoon chilli powder
½ teaspoon garlic paste
½ teaspoon cumin powder
2 tablespoons olive oil
onion salt to taste
300g (10oz) mushrooms cleaned
  and cut in half
lemon wedges, to serve

INDIANS USE A VARIETY OF MILK PRODUCTS. YOGHURT OR *DAHI* IS EATEN ALL OVER INDIA AND, ALONG WITH SOFT RICE, FORMS THE STAPLE DIET OF EVEN VERY LITTLE CHILDREN. IT IS EXCELLENT FOR THE DIGESTION AND MOST INDIANS WILL SAY THAT A MEAL IS INCOMPLETE WITHOUT AT LEAST A SPOONFUL OF YOGHURT.

Raitas are salads mixed into yoghurt. The yoghurt adds a tang and smoothness and provides a cool blandness to counteract the spice in the rest of the meal. Raitas are made with raw vegetables like carrot or cucumber, cooked ones such as potatoes or beetroot, with fruits such as pineapple or orange, or simply with herbs — mint, for example.

In south India, people eat yoghurt at the end of a meal, usually with rice and a hot pickle. In the north, it is drunk throughout the meal in the form of *lassi*, made by mixing yoghurt and water. An Indian meal will almost always include a salad or raita for colour, texture and fibre. Salads combine vegetables, fruit and nuts and are eaten with the main meal. They are simple to make, take no time at all and complement all Indian food.

SALADS
AND
RAITAS

This is a popular roadside snack in India. On their way home, office workers can be seen outside train stations eating platefuls of watermelon, papaya, chikoo (known as sapota outside India), and bananas. Chaat can also be served with any spicy meat or chicken dish

FRUIT CHAAT
spiced fruit salad

Lightly mix all the ingredients together, chill then serve.

Preparation time: 10 minutes

300g (10oz) mixed fresh fruit
   (choose firm ones such as
   mango, apple, pear, whole
   grapes, banana, papaya or
   melon), diced
¼ teaspoon chilli powder
1 teaspoon lemon juice
1 teaspoon honey
½ teaspoon rock salt

Dudhi is a long, fat pale green vegetable belonging to the gourd family. It has spongy but firm white flesh and tastes rather bland – which makes it very versatile. It is sometimes used to thicken vegetable soups. You can remove the skin, as you would for pumpkin. (Pumpkin can be substituted, but dudhi is widely found in Indian food shops.) The mint adds a refreshing zing to this raita, which is good served with meat.

DUDHI PUDINE KA RAITA

Preparation time: 10 minutes

dudhi and mint raita

1 Put the dudhi in a heatproof bowl. Pour over just enough boiling water to cover it. Sweat it for 2–3 minutes. Drain, allow to cool.

2 Combine the yoghurt, mint sauce, cumin powder and salt and beat for 1 minute.

3 Tip in the drained dudhi, stir and serve immediately.

150g (5oz) dudhi, peeled and
  grated
200ml (7floz) natural yoghurt,
  beaten
1 teaspoon bottled mint sauce
1/4 teaspoon roasted cumin,
  powdered
salt

Chickpeas are very popular in north India where they are made into a curry eaten with huge fried bread discs called bhaturas. This chickpea salad adds instant colour and texture to a meal and can make a great picnic dish with garlic bread. It is quite

CHANA RANGEELA

colourful chickpea salad (right)

Combine the chickpeas with the rest of the ingredients. Serve at room temperature.

Preparation time: 10 minutes

1 x 400g (14oz) can chickpeas, drained and rinsed

5 tablespoons diced peppers (mixed colours)

1 medium onion, chopped

rock salt

generous pinch roasted cumin powder

generous pinch sugar

2 teaspoons lemon-infused olive oil

2 teaspoons finely chopped coriander leaves

MURG AUR KAJU KA SALAAD

chicken and cashew nut salad

1 Combine the chicken, pineapple, cashew nuts, yoghurt and coriander. Stir in 3 tablespoons of the pineapple juice. Mix well.

2 Chill and add salt just before serving.

Preparation time: 10 minutes

225g (8oz) cooked chicken

1 small can pineapple chunks

100g (3½oz) cashew nuts

5 tablespoons natural yoghurt

1 tablespoon coriander, chopped finely

salt

This unusual salad introduces a smoky flavour that is not common in Indian vegetarian cooking. It is very popular amongst the farmers of western India who eat it with a fat millet bread called bhakri, some garlic chutney and a slice of raw onion. You can also put little dollops of it on top of savoury biscuits to serve as a starter or with drinks.

VANGYACHE BHAREET

roasted aubergine in yoghurt

Preparation time: 10 minutes

Cooking time: 15 minutes

1 Brush the aubergine with oil and place under a grill to roast (make sure you put a pan underneath to collect the juice). Turn it from time to time until soft.

2 Discard the juice. Allow the aubergine to cool slightly and peel off skin. This will have become paper-crisp and will come off easily.

3 Mash the aubergine flesh with a fork, then add the remaining ingredients.

4 Serve cold on a bed of lettuce, or on savoury biscuits.

1 large aubergine
sunflower oil for brushing
1 medium onion, chopped finely
1 medium green chilli, chopped
1 tablespoon chopped coriander
  leaves
150ml (5fl oz) natural yoghurt
salt
¼ teaspoon sugar

The western coastline of India is green with mango farms where countless varieties of the fruit grow. In summer, fruit pickers load the fruit into vans to transport to the cities where they are sold for high prices. The firm-fleshed, fragrant Alphonso is the king, but any number of wild mangoes, all sweet and juicy, are used in the cooking of this part of the country.

AAM KA SASAM

wild mango and coconut salad

1 Combine the coconut, chilli powder, sugar, mustard, salt and a couple of teaspoons of water to dissolve the sugar. Stir until well blended.

2 Add the mango. Stir, and serve chilled.

225g (8oz) desiccated coconut
¼ teaspoon mild chilli powder
3 tablespoons dark brown sugar
½ teaspoon wholegrain mustard
salt
225g (8oz) ripe mango, peeled,
    stoned and cubed

Preparation time: 15 minutes

Strawberries are available all over India from November until March when the weather is suitable for their harvest. They are grown in cool hill stations on strawberry farms that make their own branded jam and juice. This colourful salad brings cheer to summer parties and barbeques. The sweetness of the berries complements spicy chicken dishes beautifully.

Preparation time: 15 minutes

KA KHATTA MEETHA SALAD

berry salad

1 Combine the berries and the mustard cress.

2 Mix the ingredients of the dressing until well blended and drizzle over the fruit.

3 Serve cold, preferably on a bed of mixed lettuce.

150g (5oz) strawberries, hulled
  and halved
150g (5oz) raspberries, hulled
1 punnet mustard cress

FOR THE DRESSING
4 tablespoons orange juice
rock salt
pinch freshly crushed black
  peppercorns

This is such a simple yet popular salad and goes with any Indian meal. It is made all over India as the ingredients are universally available. It is so fresh and bright to look at, it resembles a bowl of jewels on the dinner table Any leftovers can be drained of the dressing and used as a sandwich filling.

TAMATER KHEERE KA KACHUMBER

tomato and cucumber jewel salad

1 Combine all the ingredients and serve immediately.

2 If you need to prepare this salad in advance, make the dressing of lemon juice, salt, sugar and pepper separately, and stir into the vegetables at the last moment.

Preparation time: 10 minutes

150g (5oz) ripe, red tomatoes, chopped

150g (5oz) cucumber, peeled and diced

2 tablespoons lemon juice

salt

½ teaspoon sugar

¼ teaspoon crushed black peppercorns

ALOO CHAAT

sweet-and-sour potatoes tossed in spices (right)

1 Combine the dissolved tamarind and sugar and heat, stirring until well blended and slightly thick. Cool and set aside.

2 Arrange the cooked potatoes in a serving dish. Drizzle with the tamarind mixture.

3 Sprinkle with chilli powder, rock salt and cumin powder.

4 Serve at room temperature, topped with crisp Bombay mix.

Preparation time: 15 minutes   Cooking time: 10 minutes

2 tablespoons tamarind paste or pulp, dissolved in 150ml (¼ pint) water

2 tablespoons dark brown sugar

300g (10oz) potatoes, boiled and cubed

¼ teaspoon chilli powder

rock salt

¼ teaspoon roasted cumin powder

3 tablespoons crisp Bombay mix

PANEER KA RAITA

cottage cheese and croûton salad

1 Arrange a bed of lettuce on a serving dish. Gently pile the paneer cubes on top.

2 To make the dressing, whisk together the yoghurt, cheese, garlic and onion salt until smooth.

3 Pour the dressing over the paneer and lettuce. Serve at once, topped with garlic croûtons.

Preparation time: 15 minutes

300g (10oz) mixed lettuce leaves

300g (10oz) paneer, cubed

FOR THE DRESSING

150ml (5fl oz) natural yoghurt

2 tablespoons cream cheese

¼ teaspoon garlic paste

onion salt

2 tablespoons garlic croûtons

Beetroot is a favourite salad vegetable in India and you can really see large ones in the markets. They are served raw or cooked. This salad makes a lovely centrepiece on a dinner table because of its beautiful mauve colour. For maximum effect, serve it chilled in a bow with a few purple orchids curved around the rim.

CHUKANDAR KA RAITA

beetroot raita

Combine all the ingredients, chill and serve.

Preparation time: 10 minutes

150g (5oz) cooked beetroot, cubed
1 green chilli, chopped finely
200ml (7fl oz) natural yoghurt,
 beaten
salt
1 teaspoon sugar

THE LARGE TRIANGLE OF LAND THAT FORMS THE SOUTHERN PENINSULA OF INDIA IS SURROUNDED BY THREE GREAT SEAS: THE ARABIAN SEA ON THE WEST, LAPPING AT THE BEACHES OF MUMBAI, WHERE I LIVE; THE INDIAN OCEAN TO THE SOUTH, CONNECTING US WITH THAT PARADISE ON EARTH SRI LANKA; AND THE BAY OF BENGAL — A SOURCE OF GREAT DELIGHT TO THE BENGALIS WHO LOVE THEIR FISH SO MUCH.

Every coastal town has its fish market. The fisherfolk cast their nets at night and bring back a mind-boggling variety of fish and seafood at daybreak. The biggest fish market in Mumbai is at Sasoon Dock. Trawlers and boats carrying all kinds of fish — including shark, pomfret, prawns, lobsters and crabs — arrive at 5 am. The biggest fish and the best shellfish are taken away by restaurateurs. Then the fisherwomen sort the rest of the catch by hand, put it into baskets and start to sell it. There is plenty of bargaining and, by 11 am, the fish is all sold, the market bare.

In India's interior regions, there are plenty of rivers filled with fat orange and silver fish, such as mandli, hilsa and rohu, and black crabs. The flesh of river fish is sweeter in taste than that of sea fish. The Bengalis love fresh-water fish, but salt-water species are preferred in south India.

FISH
AND
SEAFOOD

This recipe is from my grandmother's kitchen. These deliciously prepared prawns can also be bought from little stalls on the beaches of Bombay. I have wonderful memories of eating them out of little paper cones, watching a heavy sun dip into the darkening Arabian Sea.

JHINGA KURKURE
bombay crisp garlic prawns

1 Mix all the ingredients of the marinade and gently stir the prawns into it. Set aside.

2 Heat the oil in a large frying pan.

3 Roll the prawns in the semolina and place a few at a time into the oil when it is smoking hot. Reduce the heat and fry the prawns for a couple of minutes on each side until done.

4 Remove and drain on kitchen paper. Keep warm while you cook the remaining prawns.

5 Serve hot, accompanied by a crisp green salad or with plain boiled rice and Cumin and Pepper Curry (see page 106).

Preparation time: 5 minutes + 15 minutes marinating
Cooking time: 15 minutes

FOR THE MARINADE
½ teaspoon turmeric powder
½ teaspoon chilli powder
½ teaspoon garlic paste
salt

600g (1¼lb) large uncooked
  prawns, shelled
sunflower oil for shallow-frying
6 tablespoons semolina

Although shellfish abounds in the coastal waters around India, prawns are a national favourite. Some varieties can be up to 20cm (8 inches) long. This recipe is for an exotic-looking dish full of flavour and zing. Enjoy it on its own or with naan or roti to soak up the delicious coriander sauce.

JALPARI HARA MASALA

prawns in green herbs

1 Put the ingredients for the masala in a blender and purée until smooth. Reserve.

2 Heat the oil in a wok and tip in the cumin seeds.

3 Add the green masala and fry for 1–2 minutes.

4 Add the prawns and salt. Reduce the heat and cook until the prawns are done, adding a little water if necessary. The sauce should be thick and smooth. Serve immediately.

Preparation time: 10 minutes   Cooking time: 10 minutes

FOR THE GREEN MASALA
1 bunch coriander leaves
2 fresh green chillies
2 teaspoons ginger-garlic paste
salt

2 tablespoons sunflower oil
½ teaspoon cumin seeds
600g (1¼lb) jumbo prawns, shelled and deveined
salt

This dish is from south India which is dotted with coffee and eucalyptus plantations. Creepers of pepper climb the trees and fill the air with a spicy aroma. In this recipe, the piquancy of green peppercorns (I use the bottled ones pickled in brine) and the sharpness of black ones provide an irresistible combination of flavours.

JHINGA MIRIWALE

tiger prawn and pepper fry

1 Heat the oil and drop in the chillies, black peppercorns and aniseed. Stir for 1 minute.

2 Tip in the shallots and garlic and stir. Add the tomato purée and salt. Blend together.

3 Mix in the tiger prawns and toss until well sealed on all sides.

4 Add 4 tablespoons water and cook until prawns are done.

5 Serve hot, sprinkled with green peppercorns.

Preparation time: 10 minutes   Cooking time 10 minutes

2 tablespoons sunflower oil

8 dried red Kashmiri chillies, broken in half

1 teaspoon black peppercorns, crushed

1 teaspoon aniseed

12 shallots, chopped

1 teaspoon garlic paste

1 tablespoon tomato purée

salt

600g (1¼lb) tiger prawns, shelled and cleaned

1 tablespoon pickled green peppercorns

This recipe captures the laid-back ambience of Goa's sun-drenched beaches. Kebabs are popular all over India and are sold at many street stalls. The addition of peppers adds drama. Cut the peppers and onions into chunks roughly the size of the prawns. Serve the kebabs with a roti and a salad.

JHINGA KEBAB

crisp prawn kebabs

1 Mix all the ingredients of the marinade and soak the prawns in it for 15 minutes. Set aside.

2 Thread the prawns, peppers and onions alternately on the skewers until each resembles a colourful ribbon. Brush with oil. Place under a medium grill and cook for 20 minutes, turning over halfway through cooking. Serve hot.

Preparation time: 10 minutes + 15 minutes soaking time

Cooking time: 25 minutes

FOR THE MARINADE

2 tablespoons lemon juice

½ teaspoon turmeric powder

½ teaspoon chilli powder

½ teaspoon garlic paste

salt

600g (1¼lb) large uncooked
   prawns, shelled

150g (5oz) mixed peppers, cut
   into large chunks

150g (5oz) onions, cut into large
   chunks

8 skewers

MACCHI LAHSUNI

salmon with garlic crumb (right)

1 Brush the salmon with a little of the oil, season and grill for about 10 minutes.

2 Meanwhile heat the remaining oil in a frying pan, add the breadcrumbs, garlic paste, nuts, turmeric powder and onion salt. Cook until deep golden, stirring continuously.

3 Spoon over the fish and serve immediately.

Preparation time: 5 minutes Cooking time: 10 minutes

4 salmon steaks, seasoned with salt
2 tablespoons sunflower oil
100g (3½oz) breadcrumbs
¼ teaspoon garlic paste
2 tablespoons broken cashew nuts
½ teaspoon turmeric powder
onion salt

CHUTNEY NI MACCHI

plaice with mint chutney

1 Blend all the ingredients for the chutney to a fine paste in a food processor, adding a tablespoon of water if necessary.

2 Smear each fillet of fish with a little chutney and wrap individually in banana leaves or foil. Steam for 10 minutes. (There is no need for them to be in a single layer.)

3 Serve, still wrapped, although note that banana leaves are not edible. This goes well with rice and Lentil and Vegetable Purée (see page 102).

Preparation time: 15 minutes Cooking time: 10 minutes

FOR THE CHUTNEY
25g (1oz) pineapple mint leaves
15g (½oz) fresh coriander
2 green chillies
1 tablespoon ginger-garlic paste
½ teaspoon turmeric powder
3 tablespoons white distilled malt
  vinegar
pinch sugar
salt
175g (6oz) creamed coconut

8 plaice fillets, seasoned with salt

Imagine sitting on a beach with a glass of beer and a pot of this lobster curry and fluffy rice ... perfect. The piquant flavour makes this curry great for Sunday lunch, after which a siesta is compulsory! The area of Konkan along the western coast of India is well known for exotic seafood cuisine that combines ingredients such as coconut, raw mango and kokum, a sour dried fruit. In recent years, many Konkani

KONKANI LOBSTER KADHI

coastal lobster curry

1 Heat 1 tablespoon oil and fry half the sliced onions until brown. Add the coconut, stir and remove from the heat.

2 Cool the mixture slightly and blend to a paste in a food processor. Reserve.

3 Heat the rest of the oil and drop in the remaining onions. Stir until translucent then add the garlic paste. Quickly stir, then add the tomato purée, garam masala, turmeric, chilli powder and salt. Blend. Add 300ml (10fl oz) hot water and bring to the boil.

4 Drop in the lobster, bring back to the boil then reduce the heat to a simmer. Heat through for 5 minutes and serve with boiled rice.

Preparation time: 10 minutes   Cooking time: 15 minutes

3 tablespoons sunflower oil
2 medium onions, sliced
4 tablespoons desiccated coconut
2 tablespoons garlic paste
1 tablespoon tomato purée
1 teaspoon garam masala powder
½ teaspoon turmeric powder
½ teaspoon chilli powder
salt
600g (1¼lb) cooked lobster in shell, cut into pieces

BHUJANE

sweet-and-sour fish

1 Marinate the fish in a mixture of the chilli powder, turmeric, garlic paste, salt and tamarind.

2 Heat the oil in a flat, shallow-sided pan and add the onions. Stir until translucent.

3 Add the fish and cook gently, turning over, until done (about 10 minutes for cod). Do not cover, as the steam would destroy the perfect texture and consistency of the dish.

Preparation time: 15 minutes + 15 minutes marinating Cooking time: 10 minutes

8 fillets of fish
1 teaspoon chilli powder
1 teaspoon turmeric powder
1 teaspoon garlic paste
salt
1 tablespoon tamarind paste or pulp,
   dissolved in 2 tablespoons water
4 tablespoons sunflower oil
4 large onions, chopped finely

BHARLELI KALWA

stuffed mussels

1 Blend the ingredients for the masala to a smooth green paste in a coffee grinder or small blender. Reserve.

2 Heat the oil and fry the onion until golden. Add the tomato and salt. Stir.

3 Add the green masala paste and stir until blended.

4 Spoon a little of this mixture over each mussel. Sprinkle with a little cheese and put under a hot grill until the cheese just begins to melt.

5 Serve immediately on a bed of lettuce garnished with wedges of lemon.

Preparation time: 15 minutes Cooking time:10 minutes

FOR THE GREEN MASALA
150g (5oz) fresh coriander leaves
2 tablespoons bottled mint sauce
1 teaspoon ginger-garlic paste
4 green chillies
1 teaspoon garam masala powder

2 tablespoons sunflower oil
2 tablespoons finely chopped onion
2 tablespoons finely chopped tomato
salt
16 cooked mussels in shell
3 tablespoons grated Cheddar cheese
lettuce leaves, lemon wedges,
   to serve

Not surprisingly, the coastal people of India eat a diet that consists mainly of seafood and rice. This recipe comes from the state of Maharashtra on the western coast of India and is made by a community called the Saraswats.

TISRYA SUKKE

clams with dry coconut

1 Heat the oil in a saucepan and fry the onions until golden. Add chillies, ginger-garlic paste and tomato and stir until mushy.

2 Tip in the garam masala, turmeric and coconut and mix throughly.

3 Gently stir in the clams, season with salt and serve hot with rotis.

Preparation time: 10 minutes Cooking time: 5 minutes

3 tablespoons sunflower oil
2 onions, chopped finely
2 green chillies, slit lengthwise
1 teaspoon ginger-garlic paste
1 medium tomato, chopped
1 teaspoon garam masala powder
½ teaspoon turmeric powder
150g (5oz) desiccated coconut
300g (10oz) cooked clams (the
   shelled ones sold in tins or jars
   are suitable)
salt

The combination of fish and mustard is a favourite in Bengal. Bengalis truly enjoy their seafood and swear by the fish in their local rivers. They are especially fond of the rohu and hilsa and fantasize about these delicacies when away from home. I have altered this recipe a bit to make it quick and easy, but it is just as delicious as the original which is roasted in banana leaves.

MAACH PATURI

bengali fish in mustard sauce

1 Combine the mustard, turmeric, chilli powder, salt and oil.

2 Smear the paste over the fish and place on a greased baking tray. Bake in a pre-heated oven (190°C/375°F/gas 5) for 10 minutes.

3 Serve hot with rice and a sweet and sour pickle.

Preparation time: 10 minutes   Cooking time: 10 minutes

2 tablespoons wholegrain mustard

1 teaspoon turmeric powder

½ teaspoon chilli powder

salt

2 tablespoons sunflower oil

8 fillets of cod or similar firm white fish

This recipe from the state of Karnataka is for those with mouths of steel who dare to order the hottest curry in an Indian restaurant without a trace of hesitation. However, it is really not meant to scorch the palate; only to create a burst of heat, fragrance and flavour. Sunflower oil can be used if you can't get coconut oil.

AMSHE TIKSHE
fire-hot red fish curry

1 Grind the 20 chillies (yes!), tamarind and garlic to a fine paste in a blender. Add salt and enough water to obtain a pouring consistency.

2 Bring this mixture to a boil and add the fish. Simmer until the fish is cooked – about 10 minutes for cod.

3 Float the oil on top of the curry and serve hot with boiled rice and poppadums.

Preparation time: 10 minutes   Cooking time: 15 minutes

20 dry, red Kashmiri chillies (shake out as many seeds as possible)

2 tablespoons tamarind pulp or paste

2 cloves garlic

salt

8 fillets of cod, or other firm white fish

1 tablespoon coconut oil

This is an easy one-pot supper from Bengal that goes well with plain rice. Many fish-eating communities of India healthily combine seafood and vegetables. This curry is especially good for the winter because of its oil content. You can use sunflower oil if you cannot find mustard oil.

MACCHI TARKARI

fish and vegetable curry

1 Smear the fish with the onion salt and half the turmeric.

2 Heat oil in a large, heavy-based frying pan and fry the fish until golden. Reserve and keep warm.

3 Add the rest of the turmeric to the oil and quickly tip in the potatoes. Fry for 1–2 minutes.

4 Add the cauliflower and cook for a few minutes, then add in the tomatoes, coriander and cumin powders and fry well.

5 Add 4 tablespoons water, salt to taste, and bring to the boil.

6 Return the fish to the pan, heat through and serve immediately.

8 fillets of cod or similar firm
   white fish
onion salt
1 teaspoon turmeric powder
100 ml (4fl oz) mustard oil
150g (5oz) potatoes, cubed
150g (5oz) cauliflower florets
4 tomatoes, quartered
1 tablespoon coriander powder
1 tablespoon cumin powder
salt

Preparation time: 10 minutes   Cooking time:15 minutes

MEAT-EATING INDIANS LOVE CHICKEN AND PREFER IT TO ANY OTHER BIRD. GOANS EAT FIERY DUCK CURRIES LACED WITH VINEGAR AND COCONUT, AND SOME STATES HAVE RECIPES FOR GUINEA FOWL OR PIGEON. However, these exotic birds are most often associated with the kitchens of the erstwhile Maharajas of India who loved hunting or *shikar* and brought back game birds from the forest, such as peacock or quail, to roast in earthen ovens. The birds were marinated in up to thirty spices and cooked slowly on coal embers.

Some of the most popular culinary exports of India are chicken curries, among them Chicken Tikka Masala and Butter Chicken. There is nothing as wholesome as a simple 'chicken curry and rice' to satisfy one's passion for Indian food, but the full chicken repertoire of Indian cuisine is vast and wonderful. In the UK, many restaurants serve up Balti Chicken or Chicken Madras which I have never eaten in India. Balti Chicken must have been inspired by a classic dish called Kadhai Chicken. Balti means 'bucket' but every 'Balti' that I have eaten has been served in a *kadhai* or Indian wok.

CHICKEN

Unripe tomatoes are green. They are wonderfully tart and are largely used in south Indian cookery. They are often cooked with potatoes to accompany a meat dish. They impart a unique tang and colour to this simple chicken

MURGH HARA TAMATER

chicken with green tomato

1 Combine the ingredients for the marinade and put the chicken in. Set aside for 15 minutes.

2 Meanwhile, heat 2 tablespoons oil in a wok. When hot, drop in the cumin seeds. As they darken, add the onion. Stir until translucent.

3 Add the green tomatoes and ginger paste and cook until soft and well blended. Add coriander leaves and season with salt. Take off the heat and reserve.

4 Heat the remaining oil in a frying pan. When it is nearly smoking, add the chicken pieces and salt to taste. Stir till done, adding a little water if necessary. This should take no more than 15 minutes: the chicken should be fairly dry.

5 Serve a cluster of chicken breast topped with a dollop of the green tomato chutney. This dish is best enjoyed with a hot naan, a medley of steamed vegetables and a fruity salad such as Fruit Chaat (see page 26).

Preparation time: 20 minutes + 15 minutes marinating

Cooking time: 30 minutes

FOR THE MARINADE
2 tablespoons lemon juice
2 teaspoons ginger-garlic paste
½ teaspoon green chilli paste
salt

600g (1¼lb) chicken breast, skinned and cut into 1cm/½ inch thick slices
6 tablespoons sunflower oil
¼ teaspoon cumin seeds
150g (5oz) onion, finely chopped
150g (5oz) fresh green tomatoes, chopped
1 teaspoon ginger paste
1 teaspoon finely chopped fresh coriander leaves
salt

Mangalore, on the western coast of India, has produced a distinctive coconut-based cuisine that is popular all over India. This is a classic chicken curry with the fire of chilli and the sweetness of coconut. Serve it with rice, as it would be traditionally eaten, or combine it with garlic bread for an unusual twist.

MANGALORE GASSI

chicken with coconut and chilli

1 Heat half the oil in a wok and add the onions. Stir until brown.

2 Add the coconut, garam masala and ginger-garlic paste and stir until the mixture turns dark. Remove from the heat, allow to cool then blend coarsely in a food processor. Reserve.

3 Heat the remaining oil in a wok and add the chicken. Stir it around, then add the chilli and turmeric powders and salt.

4 Tip in the reserved onion and coconut mixture, add a little water and allow the chicken to cook through – about 15 minutes.

5 Complete the dish by stirring in the coconut milk. Serve hot but without boiling as the coconut milk may curdle.

4 tablespoons sunflower oil
150g (5oz) onions, sliced
150g (5oz) desiccated coconut
1 teaspoon garam masala powder
2 teaspoons ginger-garlic paste
600g (1¼lb) chicken drumsticks, skinned
¼ teaspoon chilli powder
¼ teaspoon turmeric powder
salt
300ml (10fl oz) coconut milk

Preparation time: 10 minutes Cooking time: 20 minutes

MOONGPHALI KA MURG

grilled chicken with peanut sauce

1 Smear the chicken breast fillets with a mixture of onion salt, garlic paste, tandoori masala and lemon juice.

2 Brush with oil, place under a medium grill and cook for 20 minutes, turning over halfway through cooking.

3 Make the peanut sauce by mixing the peanut butter and pineapple juice in a small pan. Heat gently, stirring until it begins to bubble. Take off the heat and sprinkle with chopped coriander, if wished.

4 Serve each chicken breast drizzled with peanut sauce, or serve the sauce in a separate bowl.

Preparation time: 10 minutes Cooking time: 20 minutes

4 skinless chicken breast fillets
onion salt
1 teaspoon garlic paste
1 tablespoon tandoori masala powder
2 tablespoons lemon juice
sunflower oil for brushing

FOR THE SAUCE
4 tablespoons peanut butter
6 tablespoons pineapple juice

KALI MIRCH MURG (right)

chicken curry with black pepper

1 Heat the oil in a wok. Drop in the bay leaf, cloves and peppercorns. Stir and add the ginger-garlic paste.

2 After about 30 seconds, add the chicken and mix it into the spices.

3 Add the turmeric, chilli powder and salt and allow the chicken to cook in its juices until done.

4 Finish by stirring in the yoghurt. Heat through, check seasoning and serve.

Preparation time: 10 minutes Cooking time: 20 minutes

2 tablespoons sunflower oil
1 bay leaf
4 cloves
1 teaspoon black peppercorns, roughly crushed
2 teaspoons ginger-garlic paste
600g (1¼lb) boneless chicken, cubed
½ teaspoon turmeric powder
½ teaspoon chilli powder
salt
300ml (10fl oz) natural yoghurt, beaten

Kashmir, the beautiful Himalayan state in north India is full of pine-nut trees. The nuts are sent to markets all over India and are used in many sweet and savoury recipes. The garnish of this dish is quite special and conjures images of dinners hosted by the Maharajas of India. Regal and yet simple, this chicken recipe can be made in advance and reheated just before serving.

MURGH NIYOZA

chicken with pine nuts

3 tablespoons sunflower oil

2 dried red Kashmiri chillies

2 teaspoons ginger-garlic paste

1 medium onion, chopped

1 teaspoon garam masala powder

1 teaspoon turmeric powder

salt

600g (1¼lb) cooked chicken, shredded

2 tablespoons dry-roasted pine nuts

2 tablespoons black raisins

handful of mint leaves, chopped

1 Heat the oil and drop in the chillies then add the ginger-garlic paste. Stir.

2 Mix in the onion and fry until translucent. Add the garam masala, turmeric and salt. Blend.

3 Stir in the shredded chicken and heat through.

4 Serve hot, sprinkled with the pine nuts, raisins and chopped mint, to accompany rotis.

Preparation time: 15 minutes Cooking time: 10 minutes

The size of India being what it is, the cuisine is varied and endless. People outside the country may be surprised to know that recipes associated with Western cooking have close cousins in the East, as is the case with this lovely recipe from north India. The original recipe was created in the kitchens of the Mughal rulers of Delhi. Flavoured with vineyard-fresh grapes, this is the dish to serve as an elegant meal between friends. You could also use black and green grapes for drama and serve this with pulao rice and Spicy Potato Mash with Onion (see page 84).

MURGH ANGOORI
white chicken curry with green grapes

1 Heat the oil and fry until the onion turns translucent.

2 Add the ginger-garlic paste and chillies and stir. Tip in the garam masala, salt and then the chicken.

3 Fry until the chicken is well sealed on all sides.

4 Pour in the yoghurt and coconut milk and heat gently until the chicken is cooked, adding a little water for a smooth consistency, if necessary.

5 Add the grapes at the last moment to preserve their crisp sweetness, and serve hot.

Preparation time: 15 minutes   Cooking time: 15 minutes

2 tablespoons sunflower oil

1 medium onion, sliced

1 tablespoon ginger-garlic paste

2 green chillies, slit lengthwise

1 teaspoon garam masala powder

salt

600g (1¼lb) boneless chicken, cubed

150ml (5fl oz) natural yoghurt, beaten

150ml (5fl oz) coconut milk

15g green seedless grapes, halved

This indulgent dish from Delhi goes well with a rice pulao or roti. In days gone by, it would be cooked in ghee or clarified butter, but now more and more people are simplifying their cooking and choosing healthier ingredients. Here, the subtle flavour of chicken is beautifully complemented by the cheese and cream with a hint of chilli to provide heat.

MURGH MALAI

1 Heat the oil and fry the ginger-garlic paste for a minute.

2 Add the green chillies, chicken and salt. Stir until the chicken is half done, adding a little water as necessary.

3 Add the cashew nut purée and nutmeg and blend. As it begins to bubble, add the Greek yoghurt and double cream. Heat through, adding some water for consistency.

4 Serve hot, sprinkled with the Cheddar cheese.

Preparation time: 15 minutes Cooking time: 15 minutes

3 tablespoons sunflower oil
1 tablespoon ginger-garlic paste
2 fresh green chillies, chopped finely
600g (1¼lb) boneless chicken, cubed
salt
4 tablespoons cashew nuts, ground to a paste with some water
¼ teaspoon nutmeg powder or grated nutmeg
150ml (5fl oz) Greek-style yoghurt
100ml (4fl oz) double cream
3 tablespoons Cheddar cheese, grated

Cardamom is a warming spice and this recipe is wonderful in the winter. Powdered cardamom is easily available but buy small amounts at a time as it loses flavour quite quickly. Better to buy whole pods which are longer lasting and powder the seeds within as and when required. Cardamom is used in many sweets as well and is therefore a versatile spice for your store cupboard. Indian Spiced Tea (see page 145) often contains a little cardamom powder.

ELAICHI MURGH

cardamom-flavoured chicken

1 Heat the oil and lightly fry all but a pinch of the cardamom powder.

2 Add the chicken and salt and stir until the meat is sealed on all sides.

3 Tip in the spices and tomato purée and mix well.

4 Pour in the yoghurt and 150ml ($^1/4$ pint) water. Bring to a bubble and cook on a low heat until the chicken is tender.

5 Serve hot, sprinkled with the reserved cardamom powder, with rice or rotis.

Preparation time: 10 minutes Cooking time: 20 minutes

3 tablespoons sunflower oil

1 teaspoon cardamom powder

600 (1¼lb) boneless chicken, cubed

salt

1 teaspoon chilli powder

1 teaspoon turmeric powder

2 teaspoons tomato purée

150ml (5fl oz) natural yoghurt

India is the world's largest producer of chillies so it is not surprising that we put them into every savoury dish! This one is a variation of a northern recipe. You can vary the amount of chillies according to taste. Nuts are often combined with chicken to add texture and flavour. Serve it with Beetroot Raita (see page 37) for stunning colour contrast.

TIKHI MURGH BADAMI

chicken with chilli almond sauce

1 Place the chicken in the stock and bring to the boil. Simmer until cooked through. Reserve and keep warm.

2 Meanwhile, purée the chillies, garlic paste, bread, almonds and coriander in a blender with some water.

3 Transfer this mixture to a heavy pan, add salt and simmer until well blended and thick.

4 To serve, arrange the chicken on a bed of rice, pour the sauce over the top and drizzle with lemon juice.

Preparation time: 15 minutes Cooking time: 15 minutes

8 chicken legs, skinned
450ml (¾ pint) chicken stock
4 fresh green chillies
½ teaspoon garlic paste
2 slices white bread, crusts
   removed
75g (3oz) almonds
3 tablespoons chopped
   coriander leaves
salt
2 tablespoons lemon juice

boiled rice, to serve

KOZHI CHETTINAD DOSA

spicy fried chicken-stuffed pancakes

1 First make the filling. Heat the oil and add the cumin and aniseed. As they darken, add the curry leaves.

2 Drop in the onions and allow to soften. Stir in the ginger-garlic paste.

3 Add the spices, shredded chicken and salt and mix well. Heat through and reserve.

4 Make a batter with the flour, salt and as much water as required for a pouring consistency.

5 Brush a non-stick frying pan with oil and spoon a ladleful of batter into the centre. Spread this into a thin disc using the back of the spoon.

6 Cover and cook on low heat. Arrange some of chicken mixture along the centre of the pancake, roll up and keep warm while you cook the remaining batter — it should be enough for 12 pancakes.

3 tablespoons sunflower oil

1 teaspoon cumin seeds

1 teaspoon aniseed

8 curry leaves

2 medium onions, chopped

1 tablespoon ginger-garlic paste

½ teaspoon chilli powder

1 teaspoon garam masala powder

300g (10oz) cooked chicken, shredded

salt

PANCAKE BATTER

300g (10oz) rice flour

salt

water as necessary

sunflower oil for brushing

This is the classic chicken curry made in homes all over India. The combination of chicken and tomatoes is pure magic. Often, a boiled, quartered potato is added for extra flavour. You can also dress up this recipe by adding a little cream, nuts or dried fruits such as apricots or peaches.

LAL TAMATAR MURGH

chicken and red tomato curry

1 Heat the oil in a saucepan and fry the onion until soft.

2 Add the ginger-garlic paste, stir and add the chicken, stirring to seal on all sides.

3 Once the chicken is sealed, stir in the turmeric, garam masala and salt. Mix well.

4 Pour in the tomatoes and bring to the boil. Reduce heat and simmer until the chicken is done, adding a little water if necessary.

5 Serve hot, sprinkled with coriander. This dish is wonderful served with rice noodles tossed with chopped coriander leaves.

Preparation time: 15 minutes Cooking time: 20 minutes

3 tablespoons sunflower oil

1 medium onion, chopped

1 tablespoon ginger-garlic paste

600g (1¼lb) skinless chicken breasts, kept whole

½ teaspoon turmeric powder

1 teaspoon garam masala powder

salt

1 x 400g (14oz) can chopped tomatoes

2 tablespoons chopped coriander leaves

This special dish is inspired by the cuisine of the Nawabs of Lucknow in the north of India. They would flavour their meats with various fruit and flower essences such as rose, vetiver, screwpine and jasmine. Sandalwood was also used to perfume some dishes. This simple recipe conjures up visions of royal banquets, glittering with jewels and brocade. Enjoy it with rotis.

SAFAID MURGH GULABI

chicken in rose-flavoured sauce

1 Heat the oil in a large, heavy-based frying pan and lightly fry the chicken legs, turning to seal on all sides.

2 Add the yoghurt, ginger, chillies, salt and cardamom. Cover and cook until the chicken is tender.

3 Stir in the almond powder. Simmer for a couple of minutes, adding a little water if necessary, and take off the heat.

4 Add the cream and rose essence just before serving.

Preparation time: 15 minutes Cooking time: 20 minutes

3 tablespoons sunflower oil
600g (1¼lb) chicken legs, skinned
150ml (5fl oz) natural yoghurt, beaten
1 tablespoon ginger powder
2 fresh green chillies, minced
salt
½ teaspoon cardamom powder
3 tablespoons almond powder
150ml (5fl oz) double cream
½ teaspoon rose essence

NEARLY 85 PERCENT OF INDIANS ARE HINDUS, MANY OF WHOM ARE VEGETARIAN BECAUSE THEIR RELIGION RESPECTS ALL FORMS OF LIFE. No Hindu eats meat on festive days or at weddings, whereas Muslims, Zoroastrians and the Christians have meat-rich feasts on such days. Meat-eaters prefer lamb, called mutton in India; only an extremely small number eat beef or pork.

There are endless ways of cooking lamb — as kebabs, in curries or in various patties. In traditional curries, 25 different spices may be used, simmered for hours to draw out flavour, fragrance and fire from each one. Today our ready-mixed spice powders, better methods of processing meat so that it cooks faster, and healthier oils mean that modern cooks can whip up nutritious, authentic delicacies in a much shorter time. I usually make my meat curries a day in advance as they taste so much better the next day. Also I make my curries in a pressure cooker which cuts down cooking times drastically. I know that many people in the West consider this device old-fashioned, but in India, every household has at least a couple of pressure cookers that are used at least a couple of times every day!

LAMB

MUTTONCHA PANDHRA RASSA

lamb in cashew nut sauce

1 Cut the lamb into strips. Mix together the marinade ingredients and soak the lamb in it for 15 minutes.

2 Heat the oil in a wok. When hot, add the grated onion and stir until it turns pink. Add the spices. Lift the lamb strips out of the marinade and add to the pan. Stir well until the meat is seared.

3 Add the marinade and the meat stock. Bring to the boil then reduce the heat and cook until the lamb is done.

4 Stir in the nut paste and the coconut milk. Heat through.

5 Serve hot on a bed of rice noodles and garnish with red chillies if desired. (You can make the chillies into flowers by slicing each one about six times from the tip almost to the stalk end. Immerse the chillies in ice-cold water for about 20 minutes, and they will unfurl into 'flowers'.)

600g (1¼lb) lean, boneless lamb

FOR THE MARINADE
150ml (5fl oz) natural yoghurt
3 teaspoons ginger-garlic paste
1 teaspoon finely chopped green
  chillies
salt

3 tablespoons sunflower oil
2 large onions, grated and
  squeezed dry
½ teaspoon coriander powder
½ teaspoon cumin powder
½ teaspoon garam masala powder
125ml (4fl oz) meat stock
250g (9oz) cashew nuts, ground
  to a paste
125ml (4fl oz) coconut milk

Preparation time: 25 minutes + 15 minutes marinating
Cooking time: 30 minutes

This is a classic recipe from the Himalayan state of Kashmir. Historically, Kashmir has been the point of entry into India for many invaders from Central Asia, and Kashmiri cooking reflects the influence of those cuisines. Traditionally mustard oil or ghee (clarified butter) is used as the cooking medium, but I have chosen the milder flavoured sunflower oil in order to bring out the aroma of the spices.

CHOKHTA
kashmiri roasted lamb

1 Put the lamb, sunflower oil, salt and asafoetida in a heavy-bottomed pan and heat until sizzling.

2 Cover and cook on high heat, stirring from time to time.

3 When the oil begins to separate, reduce the heat, add the chilli powder and continue to cook until rich brown in colour.

4 Add the ginger and a little water and cook until the meat becomes tender. Serve hot with rotis.

600g (1¼lb) lean boneless lamb, cubed

4 tablespoons sunflower oil

salt

½ teaspoon asafoetida powder

1 teaspoon red chilli powder

1 teaspoon ginger powder

Preparation time: 5 minutes   Cooking time: 40 minutes

RISHTA

meatballs with fennel (right)

1 Put the lamb mince, ginger powder, half the fennel powder and salt in a blender and whizz around once to get a smooth mixture. Form this into lime-sized balls and reserve.

2 Mix the turmeric, garam masala and chilli powders and the remaining fennel powder with 300ml (1/2 pint) water in a saucepan and bring to a boil. Pour in the oil and season with salt.

3 Gently place the meatballs in the sauce and cook until they are browned and cooked, adding more water as necessary. Baste them from time to time for flavour. The meatballs should be coated with the sauce, not floating in a gravy. Serve hot with rice or noodles.

Preparation time: 15 minutes   Cooking time: 15 minutes

500g (1lb) lean lamb mince
1/2 teaspoon ginger powder
1 teaspoon fennel powder
salt
1 tablespoon turmeric powder
1 teaspoon garam masala powder
1 teaspoon chilli powder
3 tablespoons sunflower oil

LIVER KI KHATTI KADHI

tangy liver curry

1 Heat the oil and tip in the asafoetida. Add the liver at once. Season with salt and stir.

2 Mix the chilli powder in a couple of tablespoons of water and pour into the pan. Add the aniseed, ginger and garam masala and stir. Pour in 150ml (1/4 pint) water and bring to a boil.

3 Add the tamarind and cook until the liver is done. Serve hot with rotis.

Preparation time: 10 minutes   Cooking time: 20 minutes

3 tablespoons sunflower oil
1/4 teaspoon asafoetida
600g (1¼lb) lamb's liver, cubed
salt
1 teaspoon chilli powder
1 teaspoon aniseed powder
1/2 teaspoon ginger powder
1/2 teaspoon garam masala powder
2 tablespoons tamarind pulp, mixed with a little water to soften

The legacy of the Raj includes a special and distinctive cuisine that is a unique mix of East and West. Pies, puffs and bakes are still made all over the country, flavoured with Indian spices and herbs, and sold at bakeries and small take-away shops. This recipe is so simple to make and yet tastes like a dream. I have often made it for parties, for a large number of people. Omit the lamb for a vegetarian option.

ANGREZI KEEMA BAKE

1 Boil the sliced potatoes in salted water until just done. Drain and reserve.

2 Heat the oil and fry the onion until soft. Stir in the garlic and allspice powder.

3 Add the mince and salt. Stir and break up the mince, and cook for 10 minutes.

4 Layer half the potatoes in a buttered ovenproof dish and season. Cover with the mince then a layer of cheese. Top with the rest of the potatoes and more cheese.

5 Pour cream all over the potatoes, allowing it to trickle to the bottom of the dish.

6 Bake in a preheated oven (220°C/425°F/gas 6) for 10 minutes. Serve at once with Berry Salad (see page 32) and crusty bread.

750g (1lb 10oz) potatoes, peeled and thickly sliced

1 tablespoon sunflower oil

1 medium onion, chopped

1 clove garlic, crushed

1 teaspoon allspice powder

250g (9oz) lean lamb mince

salt

250g (9oz) cheese, grated (I have used Reblochon (lovely!) Parmesan or even Cheddar)

150ml (5fl oz) single cream

Preparation time: 10 minutes   Cooking time: 25 minutes

I make this very simple curry for my family when I am feeling lazy but still want to give everyone a wholesome treat!

ITWAR MUTTON CURRY

Sunday Mutton Curry

1 Heat the oil in a wok. When hot, add the onion and stir until it turns pink. Add the garlic and ginger pastes and give the mixture a good stir. Drop in the lamb and stir well on high heat until the meat is seared.

2 Add the tomato purée. Mix the garam masala powder in a little water and pour into the lamb mixture. Swirl it around, add a glass of water and allow to cook over slow heat until the lamb is tender, adding more water if necessary.

3 Beat the yoghurt until smooth. Add to the curry and bring to the boil. Serve when hot through on a bed of rice noodles (popular in Southern India) or with naans.

Preparation time: 10 minutes Cooking time: 30 minutes

3 tablespoons sunflower oil
2 large onions, chopped
2 teaspoons garlic paste
2 teaspoons ginger paste
600g (1¼lb) lean, boneless lamb, cut into strips
2 tablespoons tomato purée
2 heaped teaspoons garam masala powder
150ml (5fl oz) natural yoghurt
salt to taste

The Sindhi community came to India from Pakistan many decades ago, and brought with them a cuisine that is now popular all over India. It is full of unlikely combinations that work well together. The caramel in this recipe provides colour and flavour rather than sweetness. Serve this rich curry with Colourful Vegetable Pulao (see page 121) or even with croissants! (In India pav or soft bread is often eaten with curries; croissants would be equally delicious.)

ALOO MUTTON SHAKKARWALA

caramelized lamb and potato curry

1 Mix all the ingredients for the marinade and add the lamb. Cover and set aside for 10 minutes.

2 Heat a heavy-bottomed pan and caramelize the sugar.

3 Add the oil and, when hot, add the drained lamb cubes, reserving the marinade.

4 Brown the meat and add onions. Stir until brown. Add the ginger-garlic paste and tomato purée. Add the potatoes and the marinade. Pour in 150ml ($^1/4$ pint) boiling water and cook until the meat and potatoes are tender. Add more water if necessary while cooking if the curry gets too dry.

Preparation time: 15 minutes + 10 minutes marinating

Cooking time: 40 minutes

FOR THE MARINADE

150ml (5fl oz) natural yoghurt

½ teaspoon turmeric powder

½ teaspoon chilli powder

1 teaspoon garam masala powder

salt

300g (10oz) lean boneless lamb, cubed

2 teaspoons sugar

4 tablespoons sunflower oil

1 medium onion, chopped

1 tablespoon ginger-garlic paste

2 tablespoons tomato purée

4 potatoes, peeled and quartered

This recipe was introduced to India by the Zoroastrians and has now become part of Indian fare. It is served along with a curry and rice or on its own with a salad or raita. I love to serve these with pre-dinner drinks. If you want to serve them that way, reduce the size of each 'cutlet'.

LACY CUTLETS

1 Put the onions, ginger-garlic paste, bread, chillies, garam masala, salt, coriander leaves and lamb mince in a blender and whizz around two or three times until you get a well-blended mixture.

2 Shape the mixture into lemon-sized balls and flatten each one slightly.

3 Heat the oil in a deep frying pan. Dip each cutlet in the beaten egg and fry until cooked through.

4 Serve with wedges of lemon and Pear Chutney.

Preparation time: 15 minutes Cooking time: 15 minutes

1 medium onion, chopped

1 teaspoon ginger-garlic paste

2 slices brown bread

2 green chillies

1 teaspoon garam masala powder

salt

2 tablespoons chopped coriander leaves

300g (10oz) lean lamb mince

sunflower oil for deep-frying

3 medium eggs, beaten and seasoned

lemon wedges, Pear Chutney (see page 153), to serve

Although this recipe from Andhra Pradesh is usually made into a curry, I have used steaks and roasted peppers for a new, almost Mediterranean twist. The mint and the peppers complement the flavour of the lamb and I often serve it with couscous tossed with a little mint.

MUTTON SIMLA MIRCH

lamb steaks with roasted peppers

50g (2oz) garlic butter

2 tablespoons sunflower oil

4 lamb steaks cut from the leg

½ teaspoon chilli powder

½ teaspoon turmeric powder

1 tablespoon mint leaves, chopped

salt

300g (10oz) jar roasted pepper
  strips, drained

1 Heat the garlic butter and oil together and fry the steaks, 4 minutes on each side. Add the chilli powder turmeric, mint and salt and stir.

2 Pour in 300ml (10fl oz) water and bring to the boil. Reduce the heat and cook until the lamb is tender and the water has evaporated. Stir in the roasted peppers and heat throug.

3 Serve hot with lemon wedges.

Preparation time: 10 minutes Cooking time: 40 minutes

In India, pure gold and silver leaf, both known as varq, are used to decorate sweets and rich rice dishes such as biryanis. They are not expensive because they are made with such a tiny amount of metal. You can find the leaf in Indian food shops as sheets pressed between butter paper. In this recipe, inspired by the shikar or hunting cuisine of the Maharajas, gold leaf is placed on top to add glamour and sparkle.

MUTTON SONAWALA

lamb with gold leaf

1 Heat the ghee or butter in a heavy-based pan. If using butter, allow the moisture to escape without burning the butter.

2 Add the meat, chilli and turmeric, ginger-garlic paste, yoghurt and salt and bring to a bubble. Reduce the heat and cook until meat is tender. Add a little water if the curry dries up. You want a fairly thick sauce.

3 Pour in the rose water and stir.

4 Serve hot with the gold or silver leaf on top. This goes well with Yoghurt Bread (see page 129) and Beetroot Raita (see page 37).

Preparation time: 10 minutes Cooking time: 45 minutes

4 tablespoons ghee or unsalted butter
600g (1¼lb) lean lamb, cubed
1 teaspoon chilli powder
1 teaspoon turmeric powder
2 teaspoons ginger-garlic paste
300ml (10fl oz) Greek-style yoghurt
salt
2 tablespoons rose water
1 sheet gold leaf (or silver if gold is difficult to find)

WALK INTO ANY VEGETABLE MARKET IN INDIA AND YOU COULD EASILY SPEND A COUPLE OF HOURS TAKING IN THE COLOURS, SCENTS AND SIGHTS. Over the past few years, an amazing variety of vegetables, now all grown in India, have joined the indigenous ones. Potatoes, tomatoes, okra, spinach, coriander, mint and lemon grass, aubergines, banana flowers, beans, jackfruit, gourds and plantains sit next to mushrooms, baby corn, mixed peppers, lettuce and broccoli which in India are considered exotic and exclusive.

Indian supermarkets cater for busy workers, selling prepared carrots, cauliflower florets or frozen garden peas and modern Indians happily stock up on ready-to-cook ingredients. Food manufacturers are just as quick to respond to the need to spend less time on our meals, so that we can use bottled ginger-garlic paste, fruit purées, powdered nuts and have wonderfully fresh paneer and yoghurt without the overnight hanging of curd or the setting of it with cultures. Thankfully, none of this has lead to any real decline in authenticity. Gourmets remain as discerning and expect the same results which can now be achieved without the time-consuming effort.

VEGETABLES

Bengalis use this combination of five aromatic spices along with mustard oil in many of their recipes. Here the mild, sweet flavour of pumpkin gets a lift. Black onion seeds are sold as kalonji in Indian shops. You can use any vegetable with this spice mixture for a quick stir-fry. You can use sunflower oil instead of the mustard oil if you prefer, but do select the red-skinned variety of pumpkin, not the white one.

PANCH PHODONER KADDU

pumpkin with five spices

2 tablespoons mustard oil
½ teaspoon cumin seeds
½ teaspoon fennel seeds
½ teaspoon fenugreek seeds
½ teaspoon black mustard seeds
½ teaspoon black onion seeds
600g (1¼lb) red pumpkin, cubed
  with the skin
salt
1 teaspoon sugar

1 Heat the oil in a large frying pan and add all the spice seeds.

2 As the seeds pop and darken, add the pumpkin, salt and sugar. Stir and cook on high heat until pumpkin softens.

3 Serve hot with Banana-flavoured Fried Bread (see page 129).

4 You could chop some red chilli over the pumpkin if you want a bit of fire.

Preparation time: 10 minutes   Cooking time: 15 minutes

Very many Indians will say that a potato subji or stir-fry with rotis is the best possible meal they could ever have. There is an amazing variety of potato recipes in every region and always at least one potato dish at festive events. This one is delicious with rotis or as an accompaniment to meat. Any leftovers can be made into shallow-fried cakes or mixed with minced meat for kebabs.

BATATA BHAJI

spicy potato mash with onion

1 Heat a tablespoon of oil and add the mustard seeds.

2 When they pop, add the curry leaves and chilli. Stir.

3 Add the mashed potato and salt. Blend well, and allow to heat through. Remove from the heat and keep hot.

4 Heat the remaining oil and fry the onion until golden.

5 Serve the mash topped with a pile of fried onions and a sprig of coriander to garnish if desired.

3 tablespoons sunflower oil
½ teaspoon mustard seeds
few curry leaves
1 green chilli, chopped
4 potatoes, boiled, peeled and mashed
salt
1 large onion, sliced

Preparation time: 10 minutes Cooking time: 20 minutes

The people of Punjab make the most divine paneer by hanging clotted milk in muslin until all the liquid has drained away. This recipe makes the most of the smoothness of paneer (Indian cottage cheese) and the tang of starfruit. Starfruit is grown in many villages in India but its blandness prevents it from being taken too seriously as a dessert fruit. You will find paneer at all Indian grocers but you could use ricotta.

PANEER TUKDE

cottage cheese and starfruit with raisin chutney

1 Sprinkle the paneer with the tandoori masala, salt and lemon juice and mix lightly. Arrange on a greased tray and place under a medium grill. Turn over when the paneer begins to change colour.

2 Meanwhile, combine all the ingredients for the chutney in a saucepan and bring to a bubble, adding a little water if necessary. When the sugar has become syrupy, remove from the heat.

3 To serve, arrange starfruit slices on a plate. Top with the paneer and a dollop of chutney. This makes a good accompaniment to Kashmiri Roasted Lamb (see page 71) and rice.

Preparation time: 10 minutes

300g (10oz) paneer or ricotta
½ teaspoon tandoori masala
salt
1 tablespoon lemon juice

FOR THE CHUTNEY
3 tablespoons raisins
1 teaspoon brown sugar
2 tablespoons vinegar
pinch salt

2 large starfruit, sliced

This is a very popular and simple recipe from Bengal. Aubergines are often fried to bring out their flavour although they absorb a great deal of oil, so drain them well to remove the excess. These crisp aubergine discs with meltingly soft centres are delicious with Lentils with Peanuts (see page 100) and rice.

BHAJA BEGUN

spicy aubergine discs

1 Mix the spices, salt and semolina.

2 Dip each aubergine slice in this mixture individually.

3 Heat the oil in a heavy-bottomed pan and fry the slices, turning over until both sides are crisp and golden.

4 Remove with a slotted spoon, drain on kitchen paper and serve at once with a wedge of lemon.

Preparation time: 10 minutes
Cooking time: 15 minutes

1 teaspoon turmeric powder
1 teaspoon red chilli powder
1 teaspoon cumin powder
salt
4 tablespoons semolina
2 medium aubergines, sliced
sunflower oil for shallow frying
lemon wedges, to serve

Makara Sankranti is a Hindu harvest festival in the month of January. Great celebrations are held in the fields and freshly roasted peanuts mixed with sweet jaggery (molasses made from sugar cane juice) and fruits of the season are eaten. Bullock-cart races entertain the guests. This is a dish from my community of Saraswat Brahmins. It is cooked as part of a Makara Sankranti feast with newly harvested peanuts. Enjoy it as an accompaniment with meat or rice.

KAIRAS

sweet-and-sour green pepper

1 Heat half the oil in a frying pan and add the sesame seeds. As they darken, drop in the coconut. Stir constantly until the coconut turns golden. Remove from the heat, allow to cool and blend in a coffee grinder or small blender.

2 Heat the remaining oil and add the mustard seeds.

3 When they pop, add the peppers, peanuts, salt, sugar, the softened tamarind and a little extra water. Cook until the peppers just begin to soften.

4 Stir in the sesame and coconut mixture and boil once. Remove and serve hot.

Preparation time: 10 minutes Cooking time: 15 minutes

2 tablespoons sunflower oil
2 tablespoons sesame seeds
2 tablespoons desiccated coconut
½ teaspoon mustard seeds
3 large green peppers, diced
1 tablespoon whole peanuts
salt
2 teaspoons dark brown sugar
1 teaspoon tamarind paste mixed
  into a teaspoon of water to
  soften

VATANA USAL

green peas stir-fry (right)

1 Heat the oil in a wok and add the cumin seeds.

2 As they darken, tip in the garden peas and stir.

3 Pour in a little water, add the sugar and salt and cook without a lid until the peas are cooked through.

4 Remove from the heat, stir in the coconut and serve.

2 tablespoons sunflower oil
½ teaspoon cumin seeds
300g (10oz) frozen garden peas
pinch sugar
salt
3 tablespoons desiccated coconut

Cooking time: 10 minutes

FARASBEE UPKARI

french beans with coconut

1 Heat the oil and add the mustard seeds. As they pop, add the cumin and chillies. Stir.

2 Add the French beans, salt and sugar and cook until tender.

3 Serve hot, mixed with coconut.

2 tablespoons sunflower oil
1 teaspoon mustard seeds
½ teaspoon cumin seeds
2 whole dried red chillies, desiccated
600g (1¼lb) frozen french beans
salt
¼ teaspoon sugar
3 tablespoons desiccated coconut

Preparation time: 5 minutes Cooking time: 15 minutes

Farmers in western India eat their lunch in the field and and then take a nap under leafy mango and tamarind trees. Their meal often consists of millet rotis, this vegetable stir-fry, a hot pickle and a knob of jaggery (molasses made from sugar cane juice) or unprocessed sugar. Cabbages have gained an unsavoury reputation mainly because they are not cooked correctly, but this fragrant dish really brings out the best in them

KOBI SIMLACHA ZUNKA

cabbage and green pepper stir-fry

2 tablespoons gram flour
2 tablespoons sunflower oil
1 teaspoon mustard seeds
few curry leaves
300g (10oz) cabbage, shredded
300g (10oz) green pepper, cut into strips
salt
2 tablespoons desiccated coconut
green chillies, optional

1 Heat a heavy-bottomed pan and dry-roast the gram flour, stirring constantly, for 1 minute. Remove.

2 Heat the oil and add the mustard seeds. As they pop, add the curry leaves. Stir.

3 Drop in the cabbage, green pepper and salt. Stir until the vegetables begin to wilt.

4 Stir in the roasted flour, crushing any lumps into the vegetables. Cook until well blended and the flour becomes mushy.

5 Serve hot, piled with coconut and a few slit green chillies if liked.

Preparation time: 15 minutes Cooking time: 10 minutes

CAULIFLOWER KA KURMA
baby cauliflower korma

1 Heat the oil in a saucepan. Add the cumin seeds and as soon as they darken, add the onion.
Cook until it is softened.

2 Add the ginger-garlic paste and tomato purée and stir. Tip in the spices. Cook until well blended.

3 Add the salt and sugar. Place the whole cauliflower in the sauce, and baste
it. Add 150ml (¼ pint) boiling water and cover the pan.

4 Allow the cauliflower to just soften but not become mushy. Serve hot with
coriander sprinkled on top.

3 tablespoons sunflower oil
1 teaspoon cumin seeds
1 medium onion, chopped
1 teaspoon ginger-garlic paste
1 tablespoon tomato purée
1 teaspoon garam masala powder
½ teaspoon turmeric powder
salt
½ teaspoon sugar
600g (1¼lb) baby cauliflower
4 tablespoons coriander leaves, chopped

Preparation time: 15 minutes Cooking time: 15 minutes

This recipe comes from Uttar Pradesh, home of the magnificent Taj Mahal. The cuisine of this state is delicate and the sweets are legendary. Here, okra is fried to a crunch. Mango powder is made by finely grinding sun-dried unripe mangoes, but you can find it in powdered form sold as amchoor in Indian food shops. Use any leftovers from this dish crumbled over other vegetarian recipes for extra flavour and texture.

BHINDI KURKURE

crisp okra tossed in spices

1 teaspoon red chilli powder

1 teaspoon turmeric powder

½ teaspoon mango powder (amchoor)

salt

3 tablespoons gram flour

600g (1¼lb) okra, sliced diagonally

sunflower oil for deep-frying

small pinch caster sugar

1 Mix the chilli and turmeric, amchoor, salt and gram flour.

2 Add the okra and toss until well coated.

3 Heat the oil in a frying pan and fry the okra in batches until crisp and golden. You may need to separate the frying okra with a fork.

4 Serve hot with a slight sprinkling of caster sugar for a hint of sweetness.

Preparation time: 15 minutes Cooking time: 15 minutes

Many kinds of flours are used in Indian cookery. Chief among these are gram flour, rice flour and wheat flour. Sometimes these are all combined to make pancakes and breads. This fragrant stew from central India is thickened with wheat flour. It is light and nutritious. Serve it with Minted Pulao (see page 122) or with bread rolls. You can add any firm vegetable you want.

SUBZION KA STEW

vegetable stew

1 Heat a heavy saucepan and drop in the coconut and garam masala. Stir for a minute, remove and blend in a coffee blender. Reserve.

2 Heat the oil. Add the onion and allow to soften. Add the chillies and tomatoes. Stir.

3 Gently mix the vegetables into the sauce. Mix the flour with a little water to make a paste. Add this to the pan and cook for a minute.

4 Add the salt, sugar and the coconut-spice powder and stir to blend. Serve hot with chopped coriander leaves sprinkled on top.

Preparation time: 20 minutes Cooking time: 20 minutes

2 tablespoons desiccated coconut

1 teaspoon garam masala powder

2 tablespoons sunflower oil

1 medium onion, chopped

2 green chillies, slit

2 red tomatoes, chopped

600g (1¼lb) mixed vegetables (carrots, potatoes, French beans, peas), cubed and boiled

1 tablespoon flour

salt

½ teaspoon sugar

handful of coriander leaves, chopped

In India, a thin version of lassi is called buttermilk. It is a popular drink in the summer and is easy to make: just stir a heaped tablespoon of yoghurt into 150ml (5fl oz) cool water. It is sometimes flavoured with flower essences or seasoned with salt. This recipe is from the palm-fringed state of Kerala where it is served as part of a sit-down feast.

AVIAL

vegetables in buttermilk

1 Grind the coconut, chillies and cumin seeds with a little water to a fine paste in a blender.

2 Add this paste to the cooked vegetables and heat for a few minutes to blend.

3 Pour in the buttermilk, add the sugar and salt, and heat through.

4 This rather thin stew goes well with plain boiled rice and poppadums.

Preparation time: 25 minutes Cooking time: 15 minutes

150g (5oz) desiccated coconut

2 green chillies

¼ teaspoon cumin seeds

600g (1¼lb) mixed vegetables (potatoes, raw banana, red pumpkin, yam), peeled, cubed and steamed

150ml (¼ pint) buttermilk

1 teaspoon dark brown sugar

salt

Indians love Mexican food and this recipe, although traditional, is inspired by that cuisine in its presentation. Crisp, tangy and simple to make, these potatoes make a wonderful accompaniment to rotis and chicken or meat. You can also serve them at teatime for an unusual but filling snack. Choose floury potatoes, such as King Edward, for this dish.

ALOO BHARVAN
stuffed potato skins

1 Cut each potato in half and scoop out the centres leaving a thick ridge of flesh on the skin.

2 Heat the oil in a large frying pan or deep-fat fryer and deep-fry the skins. Drain on kitchen paper.

3 Dust the skins with cumin powder and salt.

4 Mix the honey yoghurt with chilli powder and salt and fill the fried skins.

5 Serve at once, garnished with the coriander.

4 large unpeeled potatoes, boiled

sunflower oil for deep-frying

1 teaspoon roasted cumin powder

salt

6 tablespoons Greek-style yoghurt with honey

¼ teaspoon chilli powder

coriander leaves, to garnish

Preparation time: 10 minutes Cooking time: 10 minutes

Broccoli is a new addition to Indian cooking but its taste is ideally suited to lightly spiced stir-fries. Here, it is flavoured with coriander powder, which is made from the seeds of the coriander plant and tastes quite different from the leaves. The seeds are considered cooling and are added to many summer drinks. Serve this dish with a roti and Dudhi and Mint Raita (see page 27).

BROCCOLI KAJU KI SUBZI
broccoli with cashew nuts

1 Heat the butter or ghee and add the cumin seeds. As they pop, add the coriander powder and ginger-garlic paste. Fry for a few seconds only.

2 Add the broccoli, cashew nuts and salt. Stir and cook, adding a few teaspoons of water, until broccoli just softens.

3 Serve hot, drizzled with cream and fine strips of ginger if wished.

Preparation time: 10 minutes Cooking time: 15 minutes

knob of butter or ghee

1 teaspoon cumin seeds

2 teaspoons coriander powder

1 teaspoon ginger-garlic paste

600g (1¼lb) broccoli florets

handful of roasted cashew nuts
  (if salted, just wash and dry
  first)

salt

150ml (5fl oz) single cream

fine strips of fresh ginger, optional

The first sacrament in a Hindu's life is the naming ceremony, which is celebrated soon after birth. The baby's horoscope is cast, a name chosen and great feasting follows. The Sindhi community who emigrated to India from the region of Sind, now in Pakistan, produce endless versions of this festive curry at such celebrations. It is served with rice and crisp fried potatoes. Cluster beans are a type of long bean sold in Indian food shops as guvar, but you can use French beans.

SINDHI KADHI

vegetable and tomato curry

1 Heat the oil in a large pan, add the fenugreek seeds and curry leaves. Allow to darken. Add the ginger paste and stir.

2 Add the vegetables and pour in 600ml (1¼ pints) boiling water.

3 Mix the gram flour, tomato purée and tamarind with a little water to make a paste. Add this to the pan. Add salt.

4 Cook until the vegetables are tender and the curry has thickened slightly.

5 Serve hot with finely shredded ginger on top, if desired.

Preparation time: 15 minutes Cooking time: 15 minutes

2 tablespoons sunflower oil

½ teaspoon fenugreek seeds

few curry leaves

1 teaspoon ginger paste

600g (1¼lb) mixed vegetables (aubergines, carrots, cluster beans or French beans, potatoes) cut into even-sized pieces

1 tablespoon gram flour, roasted (see page 90, cabbage and green pepper stir-fry recipe)

2 tablespoons tomato purée

1 teaspoon tamarind paste

salt

finely shredded fresh ginger, optional

LENTILS ARE INDIA'S STAPLE FOOD, ALONG WITH RICE AND ROTIS. LENTILS ARE CALLED DAL AND DAL-ROTI IS A HINDI TERM THAT REFERS TO EVERYDAY FOOD THAT IS COOKED IN THE HOME. A modern Indian meal at home usually consists of rotis or rice, a vegetable dish and a dal (lentil) or other curry, with maybe a salad on the side.

Each region of India has its own ways of cooking lentils, beans and seeds. In the south, they are flavoured with fenugreek seeds and curry leaves, in the west with jaggery and tamarind, in the east with aniseed and onion seeds, and in the north with fried onions, tomatoes and garlic. Kashmir has the best *rajma* or red kidney beans which are cooked with only a few spices and served with sparkling white rice. In the south, black eye beans are combined with tamarind and coconut to make a tangy curry.

In days gone by, beans were mostly dried to increase their shelf life. Today, all kinds of ready-cooked beans are available in cans which do not require long soaking and simmering. Sprouted beans are easier to digest and have a better vitamin C content than unsprouted ones.

LENTILS
BEANS
AND SEEDS

Navratri is a nine-day festival in the autumn, about a month before Diwali. It celebrates the victory of the valiant goddess Durga who fought evil for nine days and nine nights during this time. The people of Gujarat celebrate this vibrant festival by dancing the raas, a folkdance from the area, and by feasting on delicious vegetarian food. This is one dish prepared for the festival and its sweet-and-sour flavour beautifully complements plain boiled rice. The peanuts create an exciting contrast of texture.

DANEDAR DAL

lentils with peanuts

1 Pour enough boiling water over the mung beans to cover them. Cook, adding more water, if necessary, until soft and mushy. Add in more hot water to obtain a thin pouring consistency. Reserve.

2 In a wok, heat the oil and add the mustard seeds. As they begin to pop, add the curry leaves and the chilli.

3 Stir in the tamarind pulp, turmeric, sugar and a little water and bring to a boil.

4 Add salt and the peanuts, allow to simmer for 2 minutes and serve hot, sprinkled with coriander.

Preparation time: 10 minutes Cooking time: 15 minutes

300g (10oz) yellow split mung beans

2 tablespoons sunflower oil

½ teaspoon mustard seeds

6 curry leaves

1 fresh green chilli, slit down the middle

2 tablespoons tamarind pulp

¼ teaspoon turmeric powder

3 teaspoons dark brown sugar

salt

2 tablespoons salted peanuts

handful of coriander, chopped

This wonderful recipe is inspired by the cooking of the Zoroastrians who came to India from Iran hundreds of years ago. It is served at festive occasions with Caramel-flavoured Rice (see page 124), a sweet carrot pickle, potato crisps and onion rings. Sometimes lamb or chicken is added while cooking. The white-skinned variety of pumpkin is not a substitute for the red here.

DHANSAK DAL
lentil and vegetable purée

1 Put the onion, pumpkin, fenugreek, mint, aubergine, ginger-garlic paste and lentils in a pan, cover with boiling water and cook until mushy. Blend with a hand whisk.

2 Heat the oil and add the cumin seeds. As they pop, add the garam masala, tomato purée and vinegar. Stir to blend.

3 Pour in the lentils, add salt and serve hot, garnished with the coriander leaves.

Preparation time: 20 minutes Cooking time: 20 minutes

1 large onion, chopped

2 tablespoons chopped red pumpkin

2 tablespoons dried fenugreek leaves

2 tablespoons chopped fresh mint leaves

1 small aubergine, chopped

1 teaspoon ginger-garlic paste

150g (5oz) split yellow lentils

2 tablespoons sunflower oil

1 teaspoon cumin seeds

1 teaspoon garam masala powder

1 tablespoon tomato purée

4 tablespoons distilled vinegar

salt

chopped coriander leaves, to garnish

This is one of the most popular dishes of Indian cookery and is served in almost every Indian restaurant anywhere in the world. I have sometimes made this in a hurry with a can of lentil soup. No one has been able to tell the difference! Here, I give the longer version. Serve with rice or roti.

TARKA DAL

lentils with onion and garlic

1 Pour boiling water over the lentils and cook over a low heat for 15 minutes.

2 Meanwhile, heat the oil in a pan and add the cumin seeds.

3 As they begin to pop, add the onion and stir until golden and slightly crisp. Remove half the onion with a slotted spoon and drain on kitchen paper.

4 Add the tomato purée, ginger-garlic paste, chillies and salt to the pan and cook until blended.

5 Carefully pour in the cooked lentils and adjust seasoning.

6 Serve hot with the reserved fried onions piled on top and a sprinkling of coriander.

300g (10oz) red split lentils
2 tablespoons sunflower oil
1 teaspoon cumin seeds
1 large onion, sliced
1 tablespoon tomato purée
1 teaspoon ginger-garlic paste
2 green chillies, slit
salt
handful of coriander leaves, chopped

Preparation time: 15 minutes **Cooking time:** 15 minutes

Indian astrology links black eye beans with the planet Venus, hence in many parts of the country they are considered to be aphrodisiacs. In this south Indian recipe, their buttery texture is combined with the smoothness of coconut milk and cream.

CHAWLI BENDI

black eye beans in coconut cream

1 Heat a tablespoon of oil in a saucepan and add the chillies, then the tamarind and garlic. Fry for 1 minute and grind to a fine paste in a coffee grinder or small blender.

2 Heat the remaining oil and fry this paste again, for 1 minute.

3 Add the coconut milk, beans and salt. Heat through and serve.

3 tablespoons sunflower oil
4 dried red chillies, deseeded
1 teaspoon tamarind paste
2 cloves garlic
300ml (10fl oz) coconut milk
1 x 400g (14oz) can black eyed
  beans, drained and rinsed
salt

Preparation time: 5 minutes Cooking time: 10 minutes

CHOLE PANJIM
chickpeas in blazing red coconut curry

1 Heat a tablespoon of oil in a frying pan and fry the ginger-garlic paste. Add the red chillies and allow to darken.

2 Add the coconut and stir until golden. Take off the heat and stir in the garam masala.

3 Grind this mixture in a blender with some water to make a fine paste.

4 Heat the remaining oil and fry the onion. Add the chickpeas and salt. Stir and add the red paste. Stir, add enough water to make a sauce and heat through. Serve hot.

Preparation time: 15 minutes Cooking time: 10 minutes

3 tablespoons sunflower oil
1 teaspoon ginger-garlic paste
6 dried, very red chillies, deseeded
5 tablespoons desiccated coconut
1 teaspoon garam masala powder
1 large onion, chopped
1 x 400g (14oz) can chickpeas, drained and rinsed
salt

MILI JULI BEANS TAMATER
cannellini beans with tomatoes

1 Heat the oil in a frying pan and add the onion. Stir until translucent.

2 Add the garlic paste, the turmeric and chilli.

3 Tip in the tomatoes and cook until well blended.

4 Add the beans, season and stir.

5 Pour in the cream, heat gently and serve.

Preparation time: 15 minutes Cooking time: 10 minutes

2 tablespoons sunflower oil
1 large onion, chopped
½ teaspoon garlic paste
½ teaspoon turmeric powder
½ teaspoon chilli powder
200g (7oz) canned chopped tomatoes
1 x 400g (14oz) can cannellini beans, drained and rinsed
salt
150ml (5fl oz) single cream

This sharp curry is from south India where it is served as a soup or over steamed rice. It is flavoured with whole cloves of garlic. In the villages, people hang strings of garlic outside their homes to ward off evil forces. This dish is often recommended to those whose appetite needs a boost.

JEER MEERYA KADHI

cumin and pepper curry

1 Heat half the oil and lightly fry the cumin seeds and peppercorns.

2   1 Heat half the oil and lightly fry the cumin seeds and peppercorns.

2 Add the tamarind, coconut and asafoetida. Stir.

3 Grind this mixture with a little water in a blender to make a smooth paste. Add 600ml (1^1/4 pints) water to make a thin curry. Add salt and heat.

4 Heat the remaining oil. Add the garlic, brown it and pour into the curry. Stir and serve hot.

Preparation time: 10 minutes Cooking time: 10 minutes

2 tablespoons sunflower oil

1 teaspoon cumin seeds

10 peppercorns

1 teaspoon tamarind paste

300g (10oz) desiccated coconut

pinch asafoetida

salt

2 cloves garlic, lightly bruised

BEANS TIKKI

potato cakes topped with red beans

1 Combine the mashed potato, salt and bread and knead together. Shape into thick flat rounds.

2 Heat the oil and shallow-fry the potato cakes, turning over until both sides are golden and crisp. Remove from the heat and keep warm.

3 To make the sauce, heat the oil and add the onion, reserving some for a garnish. Cook until softened.

4 Add the ginger-garlic paste, tomato purée and spices and stir to blend.

5 Add in the beans and salt, pour in 300ml (½ pint) boiling water and cook for a few minutes.

6 Serve the potato cakes topped with beans and sprinkled with the reserved onion. A little chopped coriander adds fragrance. Serve any remaining bean sauce alongside.

Preparation time: 15 minutes Cooking time: 15 minutes

4 large potatoes, boiled, peeled and mashed
salt
2 slices bread, soaked in water and squeezed
oil for shallow frying

FOR THE BEAN SAUCE
2 tablespoons sunflower oil
1 large onion, chopped
1 teaspoon ginger-garlic paste
2 tablespoons tomato purée
½ teaspoon turmeric
½ teaspoon chilli powder
1 x 400g (14oz) can red beans, drained and rinsed
salt

THE COMMERCIAL DISTRICT OF ANY INDIAN CITY HAS A WIDE CHOICE OF QUICK MEALS AVAILABLE ON LITTLE CARTS LINING THE STREET. EACH CART IS EQUIPPED WITH A STOVE TO FINISH THE COOKING IN FRONT OF YOU. One of the popular meals is Anda Bhurji – spicy scrambled eggs. A huge wok or *kadhai* sits on the stove, into which the cook tosses a variety of herbs and spices, onions, garlic and tomatoes and a few spoonfuls of beaten egg. A brisk stir, a wild flourish with the *kadhai* and the delicious meal is ready.

Eggs are incredibly versatile and all over India they are fried, scrambled or cooked in curries with spices and herbs. Egg dishes are often associated with the cuisine of the Zoroastrians, the community that immigrated to India from Iran many centuries ago. Their food has become a unique blend of Indian and Iranian and eggs are a prominent feature. Vegetables such as okra and potatoes are topped with a fried egg, or sweet semolina pudding is served garnished with a slice of boiled egg. Sunday breakfast can often be an omelette flavoured with cumin, onion and green chillies served with tomato ketchup and a buttered roll.

EGGS

Scrambled eggs are an international favourite. In India, this spiced version is served on toast for breakfast or with rotis or naans as a main meal. In the south, it is made with coconut milk for a creamier texture and then flavoured with green peppercorns.

AKOORI

parsi-style scrambled eggs

1 Beat the eggs with the salt and pepper.

2 Heat the oil in a frying pan or omelette pan, add the onion and allow to soften.

3 Add the ginger-garlic paste, chillies and coriander. Stir for a minute and add the tomato ketchup. Blend and lower the heat.

4 Add the beaten eggs, stirring continuously until they firm up but remain spongy.

5 Serve hot.

6 large eggs

salt and pepper

2 tablespoons sunflower oil

1 large onion, chopped finely

1 teaspoon ginger-garlic paste

¼ teaspoon green chillies, chopped

handful of coriander leaves, chopped

1 tablespoon tomato ketchup

Preparation time: 10 minutes Cooking time: 10 minutes

MASALA AMLATE

pepper and chilli omelette

1 Heat the oil in a frying pan and fry the ground pepper for a few seconds.

2 Add the green chillies. Pour in the eggs and cook, covered, on low heat until set into an omelette.

3 Sprinkle with the cheese and coriander and serve at once.

Preparation time: 10 minutes Cooking time: 10 minutes

1 tablespoon sunflower oil

3 turns of the peppermill

2 green chillies, chopped

6 large eggs, beaten with salt and pepper

3 tablespoons grated Cheddar cheese

handful of coriander leaves, chopped

ANDE KE BHAJIA

egg fritters

1 Combine the flour, ajowan, chilli and turmeric and salt. Pour in just enough water to make a thick batter.

2 Heat the oil in a wok. Dip the halved eggs individually in the batter. Fry until golden. Serve hot, garnished with a sprig of coriander if liked

Preparation time: 10 minutes Cooking time: 10 minutes

3 tablespoons gram flour

½ teaspoon ajowan seeds (ajwain)

½ teaspoon chilli powder

½ teaspoon turmeric powder

salt

sunflower oil for deep-frying

4 large eggs, hard-boiled, peeled and halved

coriander sprigs, optional, chopped

This has to be one of the simplest and most delicious curries ever. Tiny Muslim eateries serve many versions of it with fat bread rolls and an onion salad. The addition of milk or cream, if you want to be indulgent, at the end is what brings all the ingredients together in a burst of flavour and taste. I serve this curry with hot naans, brushed with butter, and Sweet-and-sour Potatoes Tossed in Spices (see page 34).

BAIDA CURRY

simple egg curry

1 Heat the oil in a large pan and add the cumin seeds. As soon as they darken, add the onions and cook to soften.

2 Add the ginger-garlic paste and tomato purée and stir. Add the spices and salt. Blend until mushy.

3 Gently place the eggs in the curry and pour the milk or cream over. Heat through and serve, sprinkled with coriander.

Preparation time: 15 minutes Cooking time: 10 minutes

2 tablespoons sunflower oil

½ tablespoon cumin seeds

2 large onions, chopped

1 tablespoon ginger-garlic paste

2 tablespoons tomato purée

½ teaspoon turmeric powder

½ teaspoon chilli powder

1 teaspoon garam masala powder

salt

8 large eggs, hard-boiled, peeled and halved

3 tablespoons milk or cream

handful of coriander leaves, chopped

This classic recipe comes from the kitchens of the Mughal kings who ruled Delhi for many centuries. Today, it is made as part of a Muslim wedding feast along with biryani and sweets made with clotted milk and decorated with rose petals. This is a pretty-looking dish that adds glamour to a buffet. It can be served with a salad and chips, as a light lunch.

NARGISI KOFTA

eggs encased in meat

1 Put the mince, ginger-garlic paste, garam masala, lentils, salt and chilli in a pan. Add 150ml (¼ pint) water and cook until the meat and lentils are done, adding more water if necessary. Allow all the water to dry up. Remove from heat and allow to cool.

2 Grind this mixture in a blender until fairly smooth. Stir in the beaten egg.

3 Coat each boiled egg completely with this mixture.

4 Heat the oil and gently lower in each coated egg.

5 Fry until golden, then remove on a slotted spoon. Cut each fried egg 'kofta' in half with a sharp knife and serve hot with tomato ketchup.

600g (1¼lb) lean lamb mince
2 teaspoons ginger-garlic paste
2 teaspoons garam masala powder
3 tablespoons yellow gram lentils
salt
1 teaspoon chilli powder
1 large egg, beaten
4 eggs, hard-boiled and peeled
oil for deep-frying

Preparation time: 15 minutes Cooking time: 35 minutes

TARKA BAIDA

indian-style fried eggs

1 Heat the oil and fry the cumin seeds.

2 Sprinkle in a pinch of turmeric and chilli powders.

3 Break the eggs into the pan and lightly stir to break up the yolks.

4 As the eggs set, season with salt and pepper and turn them over to cook the other side. Serve hot.

Cooking time: 5 minutes

FOR EACH SERVING:

1 tablespoon sunflower oil

pinch cumin seeds

pinch turmeric powder

pinch chilli powder

2 large eggs

salt and pepper

SAUCE KA ANDA

eggs in white sauce on toast

1 Melt the butter, add the flour and stir. Whisk in the milk and blend until smooth and thick.

2 Add the chopped eggs, salt and pepper and stir lightly.

3 Serve on buttered toast with a pattern of chilli powder and sprigs of coriander.

Preparation time: 5 minutes   Cooking time: 5 minutes

knob of butter

2 tablespoons flour

300ml (10fl oz) milk

6 eggs, hard-boiled, peeled, chopped

salt and pepper

4 slices brown bread, toasted and
  buttered

pinch chilli powder

coriander sprigs, to garnish

BHARE ANDE

eggs stuffed with apricot rice

1 Heat the oil and toss the apricots in it for 1 minute.

2 Add the rice and salt and blend. Take off the heat and stir in a tablespoon of the crème fraîche.

3 Fill this mixture into the hollow of each egg half.

4 Fold the yolks, remaining crème fraîche and a little salt together and pipe around each filled egg half. Serve garnished with coriander.

Preparation time: 10 minutes Cooking time: 10 minutes

1 tablespoon sunflower oil
1½ tablespoons chopped apricots
1 tablespoon cooked rice
salt
3 tablespoons crème fraîche
4 eggs, hard-boiled, peeled, halved, yolks removed and reserved
coriander sprigs, to garnish

BAIDA MAKHANI

eggs in butter tomato sauce

1 Melt the butter and fry the ginger-garlic paste for a couple of minutes. Add the bay leaf.

2 Tip in the almond powder and fry briefly. Add the tomato purée, spices and salt. Stir to blend, adding 150ml (¹/4 pint) boiling water.

3 When the sauce bubbles, reduce the heat and place the eggs in the pan. Heat through.

4 Serve swirled with cream and a sprinkling of coriander.

Preparation time: 15 minutes Cooking time: 15 minutes

4 tablespoons butter
1 teaspoon ginger-garlic paste
1 bay leaf
4 tablespoons almond powder
4 tablespoons tomato purée
½ teaspoon chilli powder
½ teaspoon garam masala powder
salt
4 eggs, hard-boiled, shelled and halved
4 tablespoons double cream
handful of coriander leaves, chopped

This creamy curry is reminiscent of lazy days beside the azure lagoons of Kerala. The cuisine of this state, situated on the Malabar coast, is rich in coconut which grows in abundance everywhere. The food is flavoured with coconut oil but the taste can be a bit overpowering for the uninitiated. Serve this with rice and a poppadum. I sometimes add a few cherry tomatoes to the curry for colour.

BAIDA MALABAR

eggs in coconut curry

1 Heat a pan and dry-roast the coriander seeds, cloves and cardamom seeds until they darken. Add the coconut, and brown. Allow the mixture to cool slightly, then grind to a fine paste in a blender, with a little water.

2 Heat the oil and add mustard seeds. As they pop, add the curry leaves, chilli powder, salt, then the coconut mixture. Pour in the coconut milk.

3 Bring to a gentle bubble. Place the eggs in the curry and finish with a couple of twists from a peppermill over the top, if desired.

Preparation time: 10 minutes   Cooking time: 20 minutes

1 tablespoon coriander seeds

4 cloves

½ teaspoon cardamom seeds

4 tablespoons desiccated coconut

3 tablespoons coconut oil (or sunflower if you prefer)

1 teaspoon mustard seeds

10 curry leaves

½ teaspoon chilli powder

salt

300ml (10fl oz) coconut milk

4 eggs, hard-boiled, shelled, halved

INDIA'S EMERALD-GREEN RICE FIELDS ARE RESPLENDENT WITH MANY VARIETIES OF RICE. ALONG WITH WHEAT AND LENTILS, RICE IS THE STAPLE DIET OF ALL INDIANS. Rice is the symbol of prosperity and many auspicious rituals are linked to it. It features in many festival menus, in sweet or savoury forms. Festive pulaos and biryanis are always made with deliciously fragrant basmati — the undisputed king of rice.

South Indians are great lovers of rice and eat it at each meal with a variety of lentil curries. To end, they mix it with thick, cool yoghurt and enjoy it spiced with a hot mango pickle. The north favours wheat. Punjab is called the granary of India because of its lush wheatfields. Most Indians buy whole wheat, clean it and take it to the local chakki or mill to be ground into flour. Nowadays, readymade flour is widely available and used by modern cooks. Sometimes rice or wheat noodles, called seviyan, are served with curries instead of rice, especially in the south. There are also innumerable pancakes or dosas that offer variety in taste and texture. These are stuffed or flavoured and served with a coconut chutney and a spicy, lentil curry called sambhar.

RICE AND
BREADS

This is a popular and festive dish from Bombay. It is served for celebrations such as weddings and at events of ritual worship where it is often enriched with nuts or dry fruit and served with a cool yoghurt raita such as Dudhi and Mint Raita (see page 27) and a vegetable curry. On other days through the year, it is combined with a rich meat curry, such as Caramelized Lamb and Potato Curry (see page 76).

VANGI BHAAT

aubergine pulao

1 Heat the oil in a large frying pan and add the onion. Stir until it turns golden.

2 Add the rice and stir until it becomes opaque, then add the aubergine, turmeric, chilli, garam masala and salt. Give it a quick stir.

3 Add 600ml (1 pint) boiling water. Bring to the boil, then reduce the heat and cook, partly covered, until the rice is fluffy and done. Add the lemon juice. Run a fork through the rice to loosen it and serve hot.

Preparation time: 5 minutes Cooking time: 15 minutes

2 tablespoons sunflower oil

1 medium onion, sliced

300g (10oz) basmati rice, washed and drained

150g (5oz) aubergine, cut into 2.5cm/1 inch pieces

1 teaspoon turmeric powder

1 teaspoon chilli powder

1 tablespoon garam masala powder

salt

2 teaspoons lemon juice

RANGATDAR BHAAT

colourful vegetable pulao

1 Heat the oil in a large frying pan and fry the cumin seeds until they darken. Drop in the bay leaf.

2 Add the turmeric and the vegetables. Mix.

3 Add the rice and salt. Stir. Pour in 600ml (1 pint) boiling water. Bring to the boil, then reduce the heat and cook, partly covered, until the rice is fluffy and done.

4 Run a fork through the rice to loosen it and serve hot.

Preparation time: 15 minutes Cooking time: 20 minutes

4 tablespoons sunflower oil

1 teaspoon cumin seeds

1 bay leaf

pinch turmeric

150g (5oz) prepared mixed
   vegetables (diced red peppers,
   mushrooms, carrots and peas)

300g (10oz) basmati rice,
   washed and drained

salt

MURGH PULAO

chicken pulao

1 Place the chicken, garlic-ginger paste, garam masala, bay leaves and onion salt in a pan with 600ml (1 pint) water. Bring to the boil.

2 Heat the oil in a large frying pan or saucepan and add the rice. Stir until it changes colour.

3 Pour the chicken and stock mixture into the rice. Cover and cook until the chicken and rice are done.

4 Serve sprinkled with the nuts and raisins.

Preparation time: 10 minutes Cooking time: 15 minutes

300g (10oz) boneless chicken
   breast, cut into chunks

2 teaspoons ginger-garlic paste

1 teaspoon garam masala powder

2 bay leaves

onion salt

2 tablespoons sunflower oil

300g (10oz) basmati rice,
   washed and drained

3 tablespoons mixed nuts and
   raisins

It is likely that the Mughal rulers of Delhi introduced mint into Indian cookery. Many home-makers in India grow fresh mint on a sunny kitchen window sill. The herb is used in chutneys and meat dishes, especially in north India. A few sprigs, slightly bruised, are also used to flavour tea. In this recipe, basmati rice gets a fresh flavour and colour by the addition of mint.

PUDINA PULAO

minted pulao

1 Grind the mint with a little water to a smooth paste.

2 Heat the ghee or oil in a large frying pan and fry the cumin until dark.

3 Add the rice and salt and fry for 1 minute. Add the puréed mint.

4 Pour in 600ml (1 pint) boiling water. Bring to the boil, then reduce the heat and cook, partly covered, until the rice is fluffy and done.

5 Run a fork through the rice to loosen it, and serve steaming hot with a sprig of mint on top, if desired.

large handful of mint leaves
2 tablespoons ghee or sunflower oil
1 teaspoon cumin seeds
300g (10oz) basamati rice, washed and drained
salt

mint sprigs, to garnish (optional)

Preparation time: 10 minutes Cooking time: 20 minutes

Tomato ketchup is very popular all over India and often takes the place of the sweet chutney that is served with savoury snacks. It is also added to chicken or meat dishes for extra flavour and is available in many forms with the addition of other flavourings such as garlic or chillies. Many enthusiastic cooks also make their own tomato sauce at home and bottle enough for 6 months at a time. Here it is stirred into a rice pulao. Seafood lovers can combine this with Coastal Lobster Curry (see page 46) for a real treat.

JHINGA PULAO

prawn pulao

1 Heat the oil in a large, heavy-based frying pan and fry the cumin seeds. As they darken, add the onion and soften. Add the ginger-garlic paste and the chillies.

2 Add the prawns and stir.

3 Tip in the rice and coriander powder. Blend and add the tomato ketchup, salt and half the coriander leaves. Mix.

4 Pour in 600ml (1 pint) boiling water. Bring to the boil, then reduce the heat and cook, partly covered, until the rice is fluffy and done.

5 Run a fork through the rice to loosen it, and serve with the remaining coriander leaves sprinkled on top.

Preparation time: 15 minutes Cooking time: 25 minutes

3 tablespoons sunflower oil
1 teaspoon cumin seeds
1 large onion, chopped finely
1 teaspoon ginger-garlic paste
2 green chillies, slit
150g (5oz) cooked, frozen
  prawns
300g (10oz) basmati rice,
  washed and drained
1 teaspoon coriander powder
4 tablespoons tomato ketchup
salt
handful of coriander leaves,
  chopped

This Parsi recipe is traditionally served with Lentil and Vegetable Purée (see page 102) and Lamb Patties (see page 77). The caramel does not sweeten the rice: instead it adds a rich aroma and colour. This meal is often accompanied by a sweet, sparkling fruit drink made of raspberries or oranges.

BROWN RICE
caramel-flavoured rice

1 Heat the oil in a large frying pan and fry the onion. Stir constantly until evenly browned. Drain on kitchen paper.

2 In a separate pan, caramelize the sugar. Pour in the oil used to fry the onions and add the peppercorns and bay leaf.

3 Tip in the rice, add salt and half the fried onions. Mix well. Pour in 600ml (1 pint) boiling water, bring to the boil, then reduce the heat and cook, partly covered, until the rice is fluffy and done. Run a fork through the rice to loosen it and serve hot, sprinkled with the remaining fried onions.

3 tablespoons sunflower oil
1 large onion, sliced
1 tablespoon sugar
8 peppercorns
1 bay leaf
300g (10oz) basmati rice, washed and drained
salt

Preparation time: 10 minutes   Cooking time: 20 minutes

This recipe comes from a community of warriors from the city of Kolhapur in Maharashtra. Their cuisine is largely meat-based and includes fiery curries and meat fritters served with a chutney made of crushed green chillies.

The combination of rice and meat is common to many countries. This pulao is flavoured with turmeric which balances the taste of all the other ingredients. Serve this dish with Beetroot Raita (see page 37).

GOLI BHAAT
rice with meatballs

1 Combine the ingredients for the meatballs and grind in a blender until smooth.

2 Form into cherry-sized balls. Heat the oil and deep-fry the meatballs. Drain and keep warm.

3 Take 3 tablespoons of the oil in a clean pan and fry the onion. Stir until golden, drain on kitchen paper and reserve.

4 Add the cloves to the oil and then tip in the rice. Fry for 1 minute. Sprinkle with turmeric and salt.

5 Pour in 600ml (1 pint) boiling water. Bring to the boil, then reduce the heat and cook, partly covered, until the rice is fluffy and done.

6 To serve, run a fork through the rice to loosen it, fold in the meatballs and serve topped with the fried onions and coriander.

Preparation time: 15 minutes Cooking time: 25 minutes

FOR THE MEATBALLS
150g (5oz) lean lamb mince
2 slices bread, crusts removed,
   soaked in water and squeezed
1 teaspoon ginger-garlic paste
1 green chilli
salt

sunflower oil for deep-frying
1 medium onion, sliced
3 cloves
300g (10oz) basmati rice,
   washed and drained
½ teaspoon turmeric
salt
handful of coriander leaves,
   chopped, to garnish

BESAN KA AMLATE

vegetarian 'omelette'

1 Combine the onion, tomato purée, coriander leaves, cumin, gram flour and salt. Mix well. Add the juice from the onion and enough water to make a batter of dropping consistency.

2 Heat a frying pan and dot with oil. Ladle in a spoonful of batter and flatten with the back of the spoon into a 12cm (5 inch) diameter disc.

3 After about 2–3 minutes, flip over and cook on the other side with some more oil. Both sides should be golden.

4 Continue to make 'omelettes' until all the batter is used up.

1 small onion, grated (reserve juice)
1 teaspoon tomato purée
2 tablespoons coriander leaves, chopped
½ teaspoon powdered cumin
200 g (7oz) gram flour
salt
sunflower oil for dotting the pan

Preparation time: 10 minutes Cooking time: 20 minutes

DHODAK cucumber pancakes (right)

1 Combine all the ingredients except the oil and blend, adding a little water until you get a batter of dropping consistency.

2 Heat a frying pan and dot with a little oil. Ladle a spoonful of batter and flatten with the back of the spoon into a 10cm (4 inch) diameter disc. After about 2–3 minutes, flip over and cook on the other side.

3 Continue similarly for the rest of the pancakes and serve hot with a spicy meat dish and a raita.

150g (5oz) coarse semolina
150g (5oz) desiccated coconut
150g (5oz) cucumber, peeled and grated
1 tablespoon soft brown sugar
salt
sunflower oil to dot the pan

Preparation time: 10 minutes Cooking time: 10 minutes

KELE KI PURI

1 Knead the flour, oil, water and banana into a stiff dough. (You may need a little less or more water than the quantity given, depending on the quality of flour.)

2 Divide the dough into equal-sized balls, the size of a large cherry. Smear your palms with oil and smooth each ball.

3 Heat the oil in a wok or a large, heavy-based frying pan. Roll each ball out into a flat disc 2.5cm (1 inch) in diameter, flouring the board as necessary.

4 Gently place the disc into the hot oil, pressing it down with the back of a slotted spoon until puffy and golden. Turn over and fry for 1 minute. It will puff up only if the oil is hot enough and the disc has been submerged.

5 Lift out with a slotted spoon and drain on kitchen paper.

6 Proceed similarly for all the poories, adjusting the heat so that the poories do not brown exessively.

Preparation time: 15 minutes Cooking time: 20 minutes

300g (10oz) wholewheat flour
1 tablespoon sunflower oil
150ml (¼ pint) warm water
1 medium, ripe banana, mashed
sunflower oil for deep-frying

DAHI PURI

yoghurt bread

1 Knead the flour, oil and yoghurt into a stiff dough then proceed as for the recipe above.

Preparation time: 15 minutes Cooking time: 20 minutes

300g (10oz) wholewheat flour
1 tablespoon sunflower oil
100ml (4fl oz) natural yoghurt
sunflower oil for deep-frying

DESSERTS PROVIDE A REAL PLATFORM ON WHICH TO DISPLAY CULINARY AND CREATIVE SKILLS. IN ORDER TO MAKE AN IMPACT, THEY MUST BE STUNNINGLY PRESENTED AS WELL AS DELICIOUS TO TASTE. This chapter shows how basic, shop-bought ingredients can be 'dressed up' to create stunning Indian confections that will delight your guests.

India has a great tradition of desserts. No meal is complete without a 'pudding', which is often served along with the main course itself. Indian sweets are largely milk-based and often contain fruit and vegetables or various cereals and flours. Ice creams and kulfis are national favourites. Lush, juicy watermelons, pineapples, chikoos (sapotas), guavas and sweet limes fill the markets throughout the year. But all Indians look forward to the summer, an exceptionally hot time, if only because the mangoes begin to ripen. Every household buys dozens of this fragrant fruit to eat on its own or combined with cream, ice cream, coconut milk or yoghurt.

The misconception that Indian desserts are too sweet is fast disappearing and lighter, healthier versions are now made in most Indian homes.

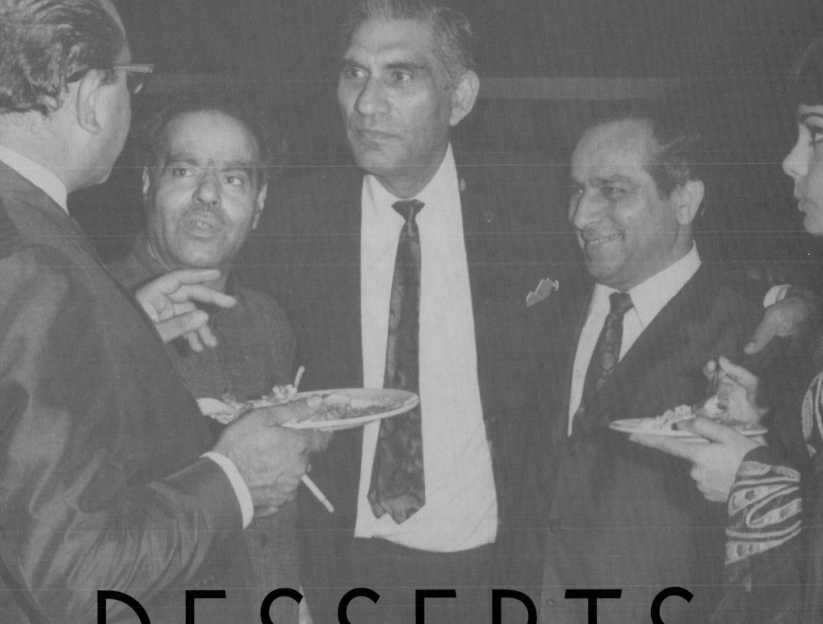

DESSERTS

PHALON KI BAHAR

mangoes and lychees with saffron cream (right)

Mix together the yoghurt, cream, sugar, saffron, milk and cardamom, then add the mango and lychees. Serve chilled, decorated with fine slices of starfruit if desired.

Preparation time: 20 minutes

120ml (4fl oz) Greek-style yoghurt
150ml (5fl oz) double cream
caster sugar to taste
½ teaspoon saffron strands, soaked in
  1 teaspoon milk
pinch cardamom powder
150g (5oz) mango, peeled and diced
150g (5oz) canned lychees, drained

KHUBANI KA MEETHA

stewed apricots with cream

1 Put the apricots and sugar along with 600ml (1 pint) water in a heavy-based saucepan and cook until tender and pulpy.
2 Allow to cool then spoon the mixture into individual serving glasses, sprinkle with almonds, drizzle the cream on top and serve chilled.

Preparation time: 10 minutes Cooking time: 15 minutes

300g (10oz) Hunza apricots, stoned
100g (3½oz) sugar
2 tablespoons crushed almonds
4 tablespoons double cream

The month of Ramadan is holy for Muslims the world over. Days of fasting end with night feasts after the moon has been sighted. People get together to break their fast with a variety of traditional dishes such as kebabs, biryanis and flower-scented drinks. This creamy, rich dessert is served at such parties. It is typically set in little earthen pots and served with rose petals sprinkled on top.

PHIRNI

rose-flavoured rice pudding

1 Mix the flour and a little of the milk to a paste.

2 Heat the rest of the milk with the sugar.

3 When very hot, add the paste, stirring constantly, until you get a custard-like consistency.
You may need a little more flour (depending on its quality).

4 Take off the heat and stir in the essence. Pour into individual serving bowls and chill to set.

This looks very pretty served sprinkled with rose petals.

80g (3¼oz) rice flour
600ml (1 pint) milk
sugar to taste
few drops rose essence

Preparation time: 5 minutes Cooking time: 10 minutes + setting time 1 hour

SHUFTA

cottage cheese, nuts and dried fruit in honey

1 Heat the ghee or butter and lightly fry the peppercorns and nuts.

2 Add the cardamom and sugar. Stir and pour in 150ml (¼ pint) hot water. Drop in the saffron.

3 Bring to the boil and add the fruit and lemon juice. Cook until the syrup thickens.

4 Remove from the heat and add the paneer. Serve warm in individual bowls, with a small scoop of vanilla ice cream if desired.

Preparation time: 10 minutes Cooking time: 15 minutes

knob of ghee or butter
4 peppercorns
80g (3¼oz) mixed nut kernels
3 cardamom pods, bruised
sugar to taste
pinch saffron
80g (3¼oz) mixed dried fruit
1 teaspoon lemon juice
80g (3¼oz) paneer, cubed

KELYACHE SHRIKHAND

banana in creamed yoghurt

1 Combine the yoghurt, crème fraîche, sugar and cardamom and beat until blended, which takes about 5 minutes.

2 Add the bananas and continue beating for 1 minute to mash them a little.

3 Spoon into serving glasses and top with the pistachios. Serve chilled.

Preparation time: 15 minutes

150ml (5fl oz) Greek-style yoghurt
150ml (5fl oz) crème fraîche
sugar to taste
½ teaspoon cardamom powder
2 ripe bananas, sliced
1 tablespoon crushed pistachios

NARIAL KA HALWA

coconut pudding (right)

1 Heat a heavy-bottomed pan and melt the sugar with a tablespoon of water. Add all the other ingredients and cook for a minute or so to blend everything together. Remove from heat.

2 Serve hot, sprinkled over a scoop of vanilla ice cream decorated with a slim, lighted candle for effect.

Cooking time: 5 minutes

80g (3¼oz) white sugar
100g (3½oz) desiccated coconut
¼ teaspoon powdered cardamom
pinch saffron soaked in
  1 teaspoon of milk
2 tablespoons pistachios,
  roughly crushed

ANANAS SHEERA

pineapple and semolina pudding

1 Melt the ghee or butter in a saucepan and fry the semolina until pink and fragrant. Reduce the heat and add the sugar. Allow to melt.

2 Add the pineapple and stir. Pour in 450ml (½ pint) hot water. Stir and cook on a low heat, partly covered, until the semolina is cooked and the mixture is dry and fluffy.

Preparation time: 10 minutes   Cooking time: 15 minutes

150g (5oz) ghee or butter
150g (5oz) semolina
150g (5oz) sugar
150g (5oz) canned pineapple,
  drained and chopped

This is one of the few baked Indian sweets — almost like an Indian custard. It is delightfully rich and indulgent, yet it is simplicity itself to prepare. The silver foil creates a shimmery finale to the meal. The foil (varq) is sold in sheets in Indian foodstores and has a shelf life of many years. (Silver foil is called chandi ka varq; the gold is sone ka varq.)

DOODH KA PUDDING
silver clotted milk cake

1 Mix the milk and sugar and heat in a non-stick saucepan until the milk has reduced by one-third. Take care not to burn the milk.

2 Allow to cool completely then fold in the eggs and cardamom.

3 Pour into a greased baking dish and bake in a bain-marie at 180°C/350°F/ gas 4 until just set (this takes about 15 minutes).

4 Cool completely then refrigerate. Serve decorated with silver foil.

Preparation time: 10 minutes Cooking time: 40 minutes

600ml (1 pint) evaporated milk
sugar to taste
4 medium eggs, beaten
½ teaspoon cardamom powder
1 sheet edible silver foil

SHAHI KHEER

crisp croûtons in saffron milk

1 Heat the oil and fry the squares of bread until golden. Drain on kitchen paper.

2 Mix both milks and the saffron and bring to the boil. Simmer until it starts to become a little thick. Chill.

3 To serve, put a few fried bread croûtons at the bottom of each serving dish, pour over the saffron milk and top with pistachios.

Preparation time: 10 minutes Cooking time: 30 minutes

sunflower oil for deep-frying
2 slices white bread (crusts on)
    cut into bite-size squares
300ml (10fl oz) evaporated milk
120ml (4fl oz) sweetened
    condensed milk (or to taste)
generous pinch saffron
2 tablespoons crushed pistachios

DUDHI HALWA

dudhi pudding

1 Melt the ghee or butter in a heavy-based pan and fry the dudhi for a couple of minutes.

2 Add the milk and sugar and cook for 10–15 minutes until the dudhi is pulpy.

3 Stir in the cardamom powder and take off the heat.

4 Serve warm, with a scoop of vanilla ice cream, if desired.

Preparation time: 10 minutes Cooking time: 15 minutes

2 tablespoons ghee or butter
200g (7oz) dudhi, peeled and
    grated
150ml (¼ pint) evaporated milk
100g (3½oz) sugar
¼ teaspoon cardamom powder

As summer approaches, a very special man may be seen on the streets of India. This is the ice-candy man, bringing a handcart lined with rows of bottles containing brightly coloured syrups. This dessert is simple to make but involves the slightly tedious task of shaving or crushing the ice to wrap around a stick.

ICE GOLA

fruit ice candy sticks (right)

1 Quickly mould the crushed ice around one end of a skewer to resemble a lollipop.

2 Sprinkle liberally with juice or syrup.

3 Present your ice candy sticks pierced into a melon and eat quickly!

Preparation time: 15 minutes

FOR EACH ICE CANDY

80g (3¼oz) crushed ice

various coloured juices, syrups or liqueurs (try rose, blue curaçao etc)

wooden kebab sticks (skewers)

AAMRAS

mango fool

450g (1lb) ripe mangoes, peeled and sliced

sugar if required

2 tablespoons double cream

½ teaspoon cardamom powder

1 Blend the mangoes to a smooth purée in a blender.

2 Add sugar if necessary and stir to dissolve.

3 Fold in the cream and the cardamom powder and serve chilled.

Preparation time: 20 minutes

THE SCORCHING SUN AND RELENTLESS HEAT OF INDIA MAKE IT IMPERATIVE TO HAVE AN ELABORATE REPERTOIRE OF DRINKS. Water is, of course, the most preferred thirst-quencher and is always served with a meal. Fruit-based drinks are also popular. The most common is fresh lemonade called *nimboo pani*, which is sold everywhere, including street stalls. Juices such as orange, pineapple, watermelon and grape are sold at juice centres where you can park your car and order a quenching glass. These centres are found in every city and town of India. There are also floral essence-based drinks, including rose, *khus*, made from vetiver, and *kewra*, distilled from the screwpine flower. The yoghurt drink lassi cools the body and aids digestion. It is served sweet or salted, at the beginning of a meal, to sip throughout, or at the end as a digestive.

India does not have a great alcohol tradition. When the Maharajas ruled, the imperial kitchens would prepare exclusive liqueurs to tempt the royal palate. These days, wine of good quality is produced, especially in the state of Maharashtra, around Bombay. However, one of the most sought-after liqueurs remains the Goan *feni*, made from the ripest, juiciest cashew fruit.

DRINKS

Just as there are juice centres all over India, there are milk bars too, selling milk drinks, yoghurt, lassi and milk puddings. In the winter, when the weather is cool enough for the cultivation of berries, raspberry and strawberry milk is sold at these bars.

RASPBERRY KA DOODH

raspberry milkshake

1 Whizz everything together in a blender until smooth.

2 Chill and serve in tall glasses.

Preparation time: 15 minutes

150g (5oz) raspberries, hulled, washed and drained
120ml (4fl oz) natural yoghurt
300ml (10fl oz) milk
honey to taste

ADRAK CHAI

ginger tea

1 Bring the water to a boil in a pan and add the ginger.

2 Simmer for 1 minute and add the tea leaves.

3 Pour in the milk and bring to a boil. Take off the heat, strain and serve, with sugar, if desired.

Preparation time: 2 minutes Cooking time:10 minutes

600ml (1 pint) water
2.5cm (1 inch) piece of fresh ginger, bruised
tea leaves to taste (depending upon the quality)
milk and sugar to taste

Indian tea is always served with milk and sugar. In Kashmir, a thick sweet brew called kahwa is popular. In other parts of the country, you can choose from the teas of Assam or Darjeeling or blended ones, for a fuller flavour. This recipe is a real pick-me-up and is wonderfully refreshing in the afternoon.

MASALA CHAI
spiced tea

1 Put the water in a pan to boil with the spices and the lemon grass.

2 Boil for a minute, then add the tea leaves and simmer on low heat for 1 minute.

3 Pour in the milk, heat through, strain and serve, with sugar if liked.

Preparation time: 5 minutes Cooking time: 10 minutes

600ml (1¼ pints) water
large pinch cardamom powder
2 cloves, bruised
½ teaspoon allspice
few blades lemon grass
tea leaves to taste
milk and sugar to taste

PIYUSH
saffron-flavoured buttermilk

Whisk everything except the nuts until smooth, chill and serve in individual glasses, with the nuts on top.

Preparation time: 10 minutes

200ml (7fl oz) Greek-style yoghurt
honey to taste
large pinch saffron dissolved in a little milk
300ml (½ pint) cold water
2 tablespoons crushed pistachios

NIMBU KA SHARBAT
Indian lemonade

8 tablespoons lemon juice

4 tablespoons sugar

1 teaspoon salt

½ teaspoon black pepper

Combine all the ingredients and add 600ml (1 pint) water. Drop in a few ice cubes serve in tall frosted glasses with a slice of lime and a sprig of mint, if desired.

Preparation time: 10 minutes

KALINGAD KA SHARBAT
watermelon cooler

600g (10oz) ripe watermelon, cubed

4 tablespoons milk

Whizz the melon in a blender until smooth. Strain, add the milk and serve chilled.

Preparation time: 10 minutes

This is a more festive version of salted lassi from the state of Maharashtra. It is usually served with all the herbs and spices left in it, but I like to strain it for a smoother drink. It is served with spicy meat and vegetable dishes or at the end of a meal, as a digestive.

MATTHA

spiced lassi with coriander

1 Grind the coriander leaves, chilli and cumin seeds finely in a blender, with a little water until you have a coarse paste.

2 Combine this mixture with the water, yoghurt and rock salt. Beat well. Strain through a fine strainer. Serve cold.

handful of coriander leaves
1 green chilli
1 teaspoon cumin seeds, roasted
300ml (½ pint) cold water
200ml (7fl oz) natural yoghurt
rock salt

Preparation time: 10 minutes

EVERY INDIAN MEAL IS ACCOMPANIED BY AN ASSORTMENT OF CHUTNEYS, RELISHES AND PICKLES, BOTH SWEET AS WELL AS HOT, MANY OF THEM HOME-MADE. Pickles are made with a variety of seasonal fruits and vegetables such as lemons and limes, carrots, turnips, cauliflower, aubergines, figs and apples. These are preserved in salt, spices, oil, vinegar or lemon juice. Each state — and each community — has a particular recipe, depending on local ingredients. Goan prawn pickle or the chicken and lamb pickles from Punjab are famous throughout India. In Kerala, pickled peppercorns feature in every store cupboard and Bengal loves its fish pickle in mustard oil. No pickle recipes are included here as they can be long to prepare and need to be matured in bright, hot sunlight — guaranteed in India, but perhaps not in other countries!

Chutneys and relishes add a sharp, pungent or hot taste to a meal. They are prepared daily, as their shelf life is limited. (In India, we use the word 'chutney' for relishes and dry or wet chutneys.) Chutneys involve grinding ingredients such as peanuts, coconut, coriander and garlic to a paste. Relishes are made by cooking diced ingredients in sugar, syrup or vinegar.

CHUTNEYS
AND
RELISHES

This is surely the most popular Indian chutney of all. It is served with pancakes and bhajias, filled into sandwiches, and eaten with rice and dal. It does not keep very well and must be eaten fresh.

DHANIA CHUTNEY

green coriander and peanut chutney

1 Grind everything in a blender with some water, to a fine paste.

2 Adjust seasoning and serve.

Preparation time: 10 minutes

large handful of coriander leaves

2 tablespoons roasted peanuts

2 green chillies

1 teaspoon ginger-garlic paste

½ teaspoon sugar

salt

1 tablespoon lemon juice

This recipe can be made up and stored in the fridge for up to three days. Its sweet-and-sour taste complements anything from barbecued meats to rotis.

MANUKA TAMATER KI CHUTNEY

raisin and tomato relish

1 Heat the oil and drop in the mustard seeds. As they pop, add the cumin seeds and green chillies and stir.

2 Add the tomatoes, sugar, raisins and salt and cook until mushy. Cool and store in a jar.

Preparation time: 5 minutes Cooking time: 10 minutes

2 tablespoons sunflower oil

½ teaspoon mustard seeds

½ teaspoon cumin seeds

2 green chillies, chopped

1 x 400g can peeled and chopped plum tomatoes

2 tablespoons sugar

2 tablespoons raisins

salt

LAHSUN CHUTNEY
garlic and dried coconut chutney

1 Heat a pan and dry-roast the coconut until brown. Add the salt and the red chillies and roast for a further minute.

2 Take off the heat, add the garlic and tamarind and blend the entire mixture in a coffee-grinder until fairly fine.

3 Store in a glass jar in the fridge.

Preparation time: 10 minutes

150g (5oz) desiccated coconut
salt
5 dried red chillies
5 cloves garlic
½ teaspoon tamarind paste

NASHPATI CHUTNEY
pear chutney

Combine all the ingredients and cook until soft and pulpy. Use on the day it is prepared.

Preparation time: 10 minutes Cooking time: 10 minutes

½ teaspoon aniseed, roasted and powdered
pinch nutmeg
3 large sweet pears, peeled and cubed
1½ tablespoons sugar
2 tablespoons lemon juice

DIWALI DINNER

As winter sets in, the most wonderful festival of lights, Diwali, is celebrated with great merriment and visual displays. During the five days of Diwali, families get together to celebrate the festival with fireworks, draw rangolis or floor patterns with chalk and rice flour outside their homes, and of course, sweet and savoury feasts. A mouth-watering feast and a variety of sweetmeats are prepared for family and friends to share. Boxes of dry fruits, nuts and milk toffees, baskets of fruit, and tins of sweets made from milk,

MENU

Poories

Aloo muttar

Amrood ka   Vali ambat   Meethi mathri
sherbat

kaju pulao

Gajar ka raita

GUAVA COOLER

amrood ka sherbat

2 medium-ripe guavas, chopped
6 tablespoons sugar
300ml (½ pint) water
300ml (½ pint) milk

1 Combine the guavas, sugar and water and cook over a high heat until the fruit becomes pulpy.
2 Strain through a fine sieve, pressing the mixture to collect as much fruit juice and purée as possible.
3 Cool and pour in the milk. Add more sugar according to taste. Serve cold.

Preparation time: 10 minutes Cooking time: 10 minutes

POORIES

fried bread

450g (1lb) wholewheat flour
1 tablespoon sunflower oil
warm water for kneading
sunflower oil for deep-frying

1 Combine the flour and oil with your fingertips into a stiff dough, adding warm water as necessary and knead until you have a smooth ball which leaves the sides of the bowl.
2 Heat the oil in a deep wok or kadhai until it is almost smoking. Divide the dough into large cherry-sized balls.
3 Roll out each ball into a flat disc, flouring the board as necessary.
4 Carefully lower the disc into the hot oil using a slotted spoon. Submerge it, using the back of the spoon, and it should puff up.
5 Turn it over and fry until golden. Remove and drain on kitchen paper. Continue with the rest of the poories.

Preparation time: 15 minutes Cooking time: 15 minutes

ALOO MUTTAR

pea and potato stir fry

3 tablespoons sunflower oil
1 teaspoon cumin seeds
1 large green chilli, slit
250g (9oz) frozen garden peas
½ teaspoon turmeric powder
1 teaspoon coriander powder
pinch of sugar
250g (9oz) baking potatoes, peeled, cubed and boiled
handful of chopped coriander leaves
1 tablespoon lemon juice

1 Heat the oil in a large frying pan and fry the cumin seeds until they darken slightly.
2 Add the chilli and the peas. Tip in the spice powders, salt and sugar. Add a little water and cook until the peas are tender.
3 Add the potatoes and stir well to ensure they are heated through. Serve hot, sprinkled with coriander and lemon juice.

Preparation time: 5 minutes Cooking time: 20 minutes

VALI AMBAT

beans in tangy coconut curry

This fragrant curry is wedding fare in south India where the meal is served on a banana leaf and rows of people sit together to eat. Professional serving staff, along with members of the bride's family, coax the guests to taste countless, tempting vegetarian dishes. It is traditionally eaten with rice.

2 tablespoons sunflower oil
¼ teaspoon fenugreek seeds
4 dry red chillies
1 teaspoon tamarind paste
3 tablespoons desiccated coconut
½ teaspoon turmeric powder
1 x 400g (14oz) can mixed beans, drained and rinsed
salt
handful of chopped coriander

1 Heat half the oil and fry the fenugreek seeds until they turn dark. Drop in the whole chillies and cook for 2 minutes.
2 Grind the fried spices, tamarind, coconut, turmeric and a little water to a paste in a blender.
3 Heat the remaining oil and fry this paste for a minute. Add the beans and salt. Stir in enough hot water to obtain a pouring consistency.
4 Serve hot, sprinkled with coriander.

Preparation time: 10 minutes Cooking time: 10 minutes

KAJU PULAO

cashew nut paulo

Dried nuts and fruit are considered luxurious all over India. The best cashew nuts come from Goa and Kerala where they are fat, smooth and shiny. Do use whole cashew nuts in this recipe as they look so much prettier than broken ones.

3 tablespoons sunflower oil
6 peppercorns
3 cloves
handful of cashew nuts
300g (10oz) basmati rice, washed and drained
600ml (1 pint) hot water
salt

1 Heat the oil and fry the peppercorns and cloves for a minute. Add in the cashew nuts and stir until they turn golden.
2 Tip in the rice and fry for a couple of minutes. Pour in the water, season with salt and bring to the boil.
3 Reduce heat and simmer, partially covered, until the rice is done. Fluff up with fork and serve hot.

Preparation time: 5 minutes Cooking time: 20 minutes

MEETHI MATHRI

sweet crunchy biscuits

150g (5oz) flour
2 tablespoons semolina
1 tablespoon sunflower oil plus extra for deep-frying

FOR THE SYRUP
75g (3oz) sugar
½ teaspoon cardamom powder
pinch of saffron
2 tablespoons crushed pistachios

1 Mix the flour, semolina and a tablespoon of oil and knead into a stiff dough, adding water as necessary.
2 Heat the oil in a deep wok or kadhai. Divide the dough into 12 balls and roll out each one into a disc, about the size and thickness of a rich tea biscuit. Deep-fry, turning over the discs, until golden on both sides. Allow to cool.
3 To make the syrup, boil the sugar with 50ml (2fl oz) water over a high heat until slightly thick and sticky — this takes about 15 minutes.
4 Tip in the cardamom and saffron. Dip each mathri into the syrup.
5 Sprinkle with nuts and arrange on a plate to cool. Serve with whipped cream or ice cream.

Preparation time: 15 minutes Cooking time: 25 minutes

CHRISTMAS DINNER

Christmas is celebrated all over India, among the Christians, as a festival of peace and forgiveness. Garlands of twinkling lights, Christmas trees and lanterns in the shape of a star, decorate each home. Many tree-lined avenues are lit up and cardboard cutouts of Santa Claus, reindeer lure shoppers into department stores. The air is full of festive cheer even though there is neither snow nor cold winter breezes here. India enjoys a warm, tropical Christmas and party-goers can be seen wearing skimpy, summery clothes!

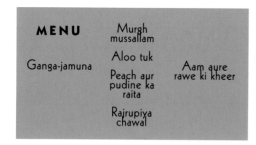

MENU

Ganga-jamuna

Murgh mussallam

Aloo tuk

Peach aur pudine ka raita

Aam aure rawe ki kheer

Rajrupiya chawal

GANGA-JAMUNA

fruit juice medley

300ml (10fl oz) orange juice
300ml (10fl oz) pineapple juice
½ teaspoon rock salt
½ teaspoon roasted cumin powder

1 Combine all the ingredients and serve chilled with a sprig of mint if desired.

Preparation time: 10 minutes

MURGH MUSSALLAM

whole roasted chicken with dried fruit and spices

1 corn-fed chicken (about 1.4 kg/3lb)

FOR THE MARINADE
150ml (5fl oz) natural yoghurt
2 teaspoons ginger-garlic paste
salt
3 tablespoons lemon juice
2 teaspoons chilli powder
2 teaspoons garam masala powder
75g (3oz) desiccated coconut
75g (3oz) almond powder
3 tablespoons apple sauce
¼ teaspoon saffron
ghee for basting

1 Make cuts in the chicken. Combine all the ingredients for the marinade and spread over the chicken. Marinate for as long as you can or up to 2 hours.

2 Blend the coconut, almond powder, apple sauce and saffron to a paste with a little water.
3 Smear the coconut mixture all over the chicken. Adjust seasoning. Place in a roasting tray, dot with ghee and roast at 190°C/375°F/gas 5 until done. Baste occasionally to keep it from drying. Serve hot.

Preparation time: 15 minutes + at least 2 hours marinating Cooking time: 45 minutes

ALOO TUK

crispy fried tangy ptatoes

sunflower oil for deep-frying
300g (10oz) potato wedges, skin on
rock salt
generous pinch of chilli powder
generous pinch of roasted cumin powder
generous pinch of mango powder (amchoor)

1 Heat the oil and fry the potato wedges until golden.

2 Sprinkle liberally with salt and spices and serve hot.

Preparation time: 10 minutes Cooking time: 15 minutes

PEACH AUR PAUDINE KA RAITA

peach and miny yoghurt

A spicy meat dish is delicious when set off by a cool, fruity accompaniment. Here the combination of peach and mint is exotic and unusual. Peaches grow in the cool orchards of north India and are sold boxed all over the country. For this Christmas menu, I have used canned peaches. You could use fresh, ripe ones if making this in the summer.

1 small can peach slices, drained, juice reserved   [size needs to be checked]
150ml (5fl oz) natural yoghurt
salt
2 tablespoons chopped fresh mint leaves
½ teaspoon roasted cumin powder

1 Combine the peach slices, yoghurt, salt and mint leaves. Stir in 3 tablespoons of reserved peach juice and serve with a sprinkling of roasted cumin powder.

Preparation time: 10 minutes

RAJRUPIYA CHAWAL

gold and silver rice

India is a land of colour and the national favourites are gold and silver. During all celebrations, traditional delicacies are served on carved silver platters. At weddings, the hall is decorated with gold, saffron and crimson flowers, interlaced with green mango leaves.

2 tablespoons ghee
½ teaspoon cumin seeds
a few mushrooms, sliced
300g (10oz) basmati rice, washed and drained
½ teaspoon salt
1 teaspoon turmeric powder
600ml (1pint) hot water
1 sheet edible silver foil (varq)

1 Heat the ghee in a heavy-bottomed pan and fry the cumin seeds until they begin to darken.
2 Add the mushrooms. Tip in the rice, salt and turmeric. Stir to blend.
3 Pour in the hot water, stir and bring to the boil. Reduce heat and simmer, partially covered until done.
4 Serve hot decorated with a sheet of varq or edible silver foil.

Preparation time: 5 minutes Cooking time: 25 minutes

AAM AURE RAWRE KI KHEER

warm semolina custard with mango

A spicy meat dish is delicious when set off by a cool, fruity accompaniment. Here the combination of peach and mint is exotic and unusual. Peaches grow in the cool orchards of north India and are sold boxed all over the country. For this Christmas menu, I have used canned peaches. You could use fresh, ripe ones if making this in the summer.

knob of butter
5 tablespoons semolina
300ml (½ pint) water
sugar to taste
200ml (7fl oz) coconut milk
pinch of powdered cardamon
8 tablespoons canned mango pulp

1 Heat the butter and fry the semolina for a few minutes. Pour in the water and cook semolina. Add the sugar.
2 Take off the heat and stir in the coconut milk and the cardamom.
3 Pour into individual stemmed glasses and allow to set for a couple of minutes.
4 Top the custard with some mango purée and serve warm. This dessert tastes lovely cold too.

Preparation time: 5 minutes Cooking time: 15 minutes

HOLI MENU

Around the time of the vernal equinox, the festival of Holi heralds the arrival of spring. It is celebrated by lighting bonfires that signify the destruction of evil and by throwing colour on each other in a ritual of rejuvenation and joy. This custom celebrates the story of how the god Krishna played Holi with his friends drenching them in colours, made from wild flowers and fruit. Merry-makers drink an intoxicant called bhang and urge hesitant friends to join in the fun. This menu has all the colours to celebrate the spirit of Holi.

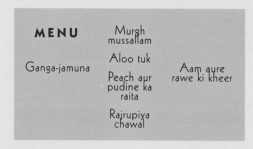

MENU

Ganga-jamuna

Murgh mussallam

Aloo tuk

Peach aur pudine ka raita

Rajrupiya chawal

Aam aure rawe ki kheer

LASSI MAYUR

rainbox lassi

500ml (18fl oz) thick natural yoghurt
6 tablespoons water
sugar to taste
2 teaspoons coloured sugar, to garnish

1 Put the yoghurt, water and sugar into a blender and whizz until blended and frothy.
2 Pour into four glasses and gently place half a teaspoonful of coloured sugar on top of each one.
3 The lassi must be thick enough to hold the sugar on top.

Preparation time: 15 minutes

PALAK POORI

spinach bread

450g (1lb) wholewheat flour
1 tablespoon sunflower oil
4 tablespoons canned spinach purée
pinch of salt
warm water for kneading
sunflower oil for deep-frying

1 Combine the flour, 1 tablespoon of oil, spinach purée and salt. Pour in the water a little at a time and knead into a stiff dough.
2 Heat the oil in a kadhai or deep wok. Shape the dough into even-sized balls.
3 Roll each ball into a flat disc on a floured board. Shake off excess flour and fry the disc or poorie in the hot oil, submerging it with the back of a slotted spoon so that it puffs up. Turn over and cook for minute. Remove and drain on kitchen paper.
4 Proceed similarly for the rest of the poories. Serve hot.

Preparation time: 15 minutes   Cooking time: 20

LAL SIMLA AUR BABY CORN KI SUBZI

red pepper and baby corn

2 tablespoons sunflower oil
½ teaspoon cumin seeds
1 medium onion, sliced
2 tomatoes, quartered
½ teaspoon turmeric powder
½ teaspoon chilli powder
300g (10oz) red pepper, deseeded and sliced
100g (3½ oz) baby corn, each cut in half
handful of coriander leaves, chopped

1 Heat the oil and add the cumin seeds. Allow to darken. Add the onion and soften.
2 Add the tomatoes, spice powders and salt and cook until slightly pulpy.
3 Add the vegetables. Stir, cover and cook until the peppers are just beginning to wilt. Serve sprinkled with coriander leaves.

Preparation time: 10 minutes   Cooking time: 15 minutes

PAPITA TARBOOZ KA CHAAT

papaya and melon salad

Both these orange fruits bring fragrance and flavour to the table. Their colour evokes the saffron powder that people throw on each to celebrate the festival. This is made from bright orange kesariya flowers.
Choose ripe fruit that is firm to touch.

150g (5oz) papaya, cubed
150g (5oz) pink melon, cubed
1 tablespoon lemon juice
rock salt
handful of orange geranium flowers to garnish (optional)

1 Gently combine the papaya, melon, lemon juice and salt.
2 Serve sprinkled with the geranium flowers, if desired.

Preparation time: 15 minutes

BHINDI KADHI

okra in yoghurt curry

sunflower oil for deep-frying
150g (5oz) baby okra, with tops snipped off
salt
300ml (10fl oz) natural yoghurt
4 tablespoons sugar
½ teaspoons fenugreek seeds
6 cloves
black peppercorns
10 curry leaves
3 dried red chillies

1 Heat the oil in a deep wok or kadhai and fry the okra until crisp. Drain on kitchen paper, sprinkle with salt and reserve.
2 Whisk together the yoghurt, flour, sugar and salt along enough water to make a pouring consistency.
3 Cook this, stirring constantly until thick and creamy. Do not allow the yoghurt to curdle. Simply whisk the sauce if this happens.
4 Heat 3 tablespoons of the oil in a small pan and add the fenugreek seeds, cloves and peppercorns. Allow to darken. Add the curry leaves and chillies and pour into the yoghurt sauce.
5 Serve the sauce in

Preparation time: 5 minutes Cooking time: 25 minutes

CHAVAL KA PAYAS

rich rice pudding

A spicy meat dish is delicious when set off by a cool, fruity accompaniment. Here the combination of peach and mint is exotic and unusual. Peaches grow in the cool orchards of north India and are sold boxed all over the country. For this Christmas menu, I have used canned peaches. You could use fresh, ripe ones if making this in the summer.

100g (3½ oz) basmati rice, washed and drained
600ml (1 pint) milk
300ml (½ pint) evaporated milk
4 tablespoons almond powder
sugar to taste
½ teaspoon cardamom powder
edible food colour as required

1 Bring the rice to the boil with the milk. Reduce heat and simmer until soft. Mash slightly with a whisk.
2 Pour in the evaporated milk, add almond powder and sugar and heat through.
3 Take off the heat and stir in the cardamom powder. Divide into four serving bowls and swirl a different shade of food colour in each one. You can also layer the different colours in each bowl for a rainbow effect. Serve cold.

Preparation time: 15 minutes Cooking time: 15 minutes

INDEX